Franz Ferdinand

jacqueline 4

tell her tonight 15

take me out 20

the dark of the matinée 30

auf achse 43

cheating on you 66

this fire 50

darts of pleasure 58

michael 73

come on home 82

40' 90

guitar tablature explained 2

Exclusive distributors:
Music Sales Limited
Distribution Centre, Newmarket Road,
Bury St Edmunds, Suffolk, IP33 3YB, England.
Music Sales Pty Limited
120 Rothschild Avenue, Rosebery, NSW 2018, Australia.

Order No. AM980177
ISBN 1-84449-521-3
This book © Copyright 2004 by Wise Publications.

Unauthorised reproduction of any part of this publication by any means including photocopying is an infringement of copyright.

Music arrangements by Martin Shellard.
Music processed by Paul Ewers Music Design.

Printed in the United Kingdom.

Your Guarantee of Quality:

As publishers, we strive to produce every book to the highest commercial standards.

While endeavouring to retain the original running order of the recorded album, the book has been carefully designed to minimise awkward page turns and to make playing from it a real pleasure.

Particular care has been given to specifying acid-free, neutral-sized paper made from pulps which have not been elemental chlorine bleached.

This pulp is from farmed sustainable forests and was produced with special regard for the environment.

Throughout, the printing and binding have been planned to ensure a sturdy, attractive publication which should give years of enjoyment.

If your copy fails to meet our high standards, please inform us and we will gladly replace it.

www.musicsales.com

This publication is not authorised for sale
in the United States of America and/or Canada

UNIVERSAL

**UNIVERSAL MUSIC
PUBLISHING GROUP**

guitar tablature explained

Guitar music can be notated in three different ways: on a musical stave, in tablature, and in rhythm slashes.

RHYTHM SLASHES are written above the stave. Strum chords in the rhythm indicated. Round noteheads indicate single notes.

THE MUSICAL STAVE shows pitches and rhythms and is divided by lines into bars. Pitches are named after the first seven letters of the alphabet.

TABLATURE graphically represents the guitar fingerboard. Each horizontal line represents a string, and each number represents a fret.

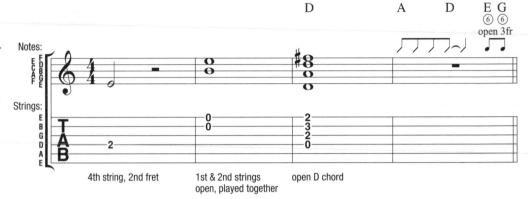

4th string, 2nd fret   1st & 2nd strings open, played together   open D chord

definitions for special guitar notation

SEMI-TONE BEND: Strike the note and bend up a semi-tone (1/2 step).

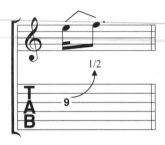

WHOLE-TONE BEND: Strike the note and bend up a whole-tone (whole step).

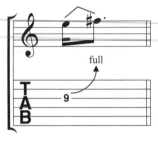

GRACE NOTE BEND: Strike the note and bend as indicated. Play the first note as quickly as possible.

QUARTER-TONE BEND: Strike the note and bend up a 1/4 step.

BEND & RELEASE: Strike the note and bend up as indicated, then release back to the original note.

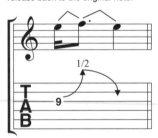

COMPOUND BEND & RELEASE: Strike the note and bend up and down in the rhythm indicated.

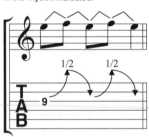

PRE-BEND: Bend the note as indicated, then strike it.

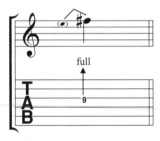

PRE-BEND & RELEASE: Bend the note as indicated. Strike it and release the note back to the original pitch.

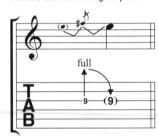

UNISON BEND: Strike the two notes simultaneously and bend the lower note up to the pitch of the higher.

BEND & RESTRIKE: Strike the note and bend as indicated then restrike the string where the symbol occurs.

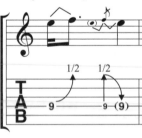

BEND, HOLD AND RELEASE: Same as bend and release but hold the bend for the duration of the tie.

BEND AND TAP: Bend the note as indicated and tap the higher fret while still holding the bend.

VIBRATO: The string is vibrated by rapidly bending and releasing the note with the fretting hand.

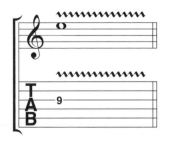

HAMMER-ON: Strike the first note with one finger, then sound the second note (on the same string) with another finger by fretting it without picking.

PULL-OFF: Place both fingers on the notes to be sounded, strike the first note and without picking, pull the finger off to sound the second note.

LEGATO SLIDE (GLISS): Strike the first note and then slide the same fret-hand finger up or down to the second note. The second note is not struck.

NOTE: The speed of any bend is indicated by the music notation and tempo.

SHIFT SLIDE (GLISS & RESTRIKE): Same as legato slide, except the second note is struck.

TRILL: Very rapidly alternate between the notes indicated by continuously hammering on and pulling off.

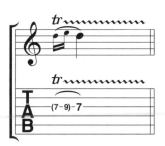

TAPPING: Hammer ("tap") the fret indicated with the pick-hand index or middle finger and pull off to the note fretted by the fret hand.

PICK SCRAPE: The edge of the pick is rubbed down (or up) the string, producing a scratchy sound.

MUFFLED STRINGS: A percussive sound is produced by laying the fret hand across the string(s) without depressing, and striking them with the pick hand.

NATURAL HARMONIC: Strike the note while the fret-hand lightly touches the string directly over the fret indicated.

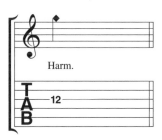

PINCH HARMONIC: The note is fretted normally and a harmonic is produced by adding the edge of the thumb or the tip of the index finger of the pick hand to the normal pick attack.

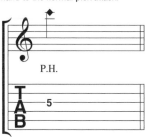

HARP HARMONIC: The note is fretted normally and a harmonic is produced by gently resting the pick hand's index finger directly above the indicated fret (in brackets) while plucking the appropriate string.

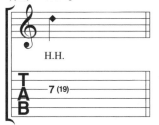

PALM MUTING: The note is partially muted by the pick hand lightly touching the string(s) just before the bridge.

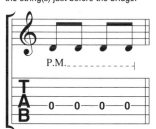

RAKE: Drag the pick across the strings indicated with a single motion.

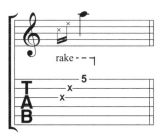

TREMOLO PICKING: The note is picked as rapidly and continuously as possible.

ARPEGGIATE: Play the notes of the chord indicated by quickly rolling them from bottom to top.

SWEEP PICKING: Rhythmic downstroke and/or upstroke motion across the strings.

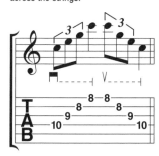

VIBRATO DIVE BAR AND RETURN: The pitch of the note or chord is dropped a specific number of steps (in rhythm) then returned to the original pitch.

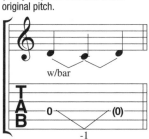

VIBRATO BAR SCOOP: Depress the bar just before striking the note, then quickly release the bar.

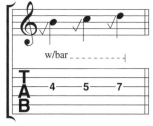

VIBRATO BAR DIP: Strike the note and then immediately drop a specific number of steps, then release back to the original pitch.

additional musical definitions

 (accent) • Accentuate note (play it louder).

 (accent) • Accentuate note with great intensity.

 (staccato) • Shorten time value of note.

⊓ • Downstroke

V • Upstroke

D.%. al Coda • Go back to the sign (%), then play until the bar marked ***To Coda*** ⊕ then skip to the section marked ⊕ ***Coda***.

D.C. al Fine • Go back to the beginning of the song and play until the bar marked ***Fine***.

tacet • Instrument is silent (drops out).

 • Repeat bars between signs.

 • When a repeated section has different endings, play the first ending only the first time and the second ending only the second time.

NOTE: Tablature numbers in brackets mean:
1. The note is sustained, but a new articulation (such as hammer on or slide) begins.
2. A note may be fretted but not necessarily played.

jacqueline

Words & Music by Alexander Kapranos, Nicholas McCarthy & Robert Hardy

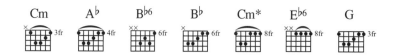

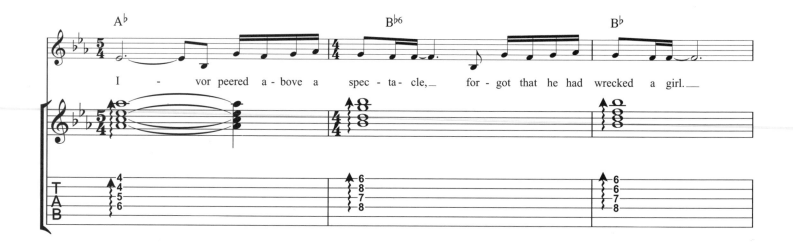

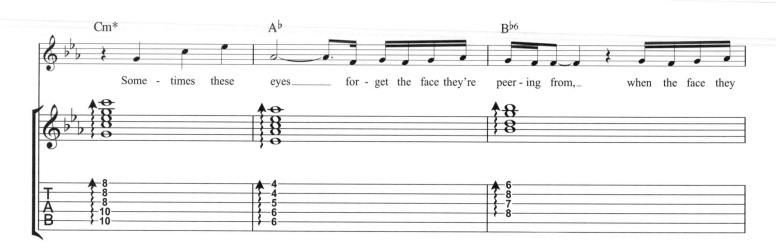

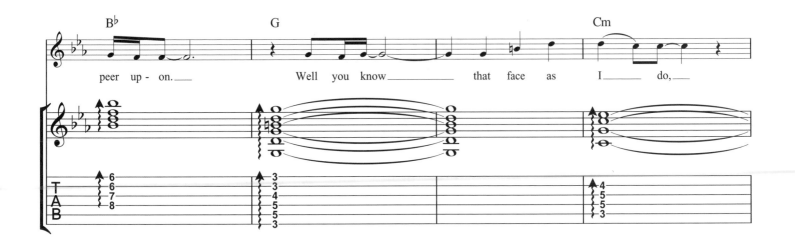

peer up - on. ___ Well you know ___ that face as I ___ do,

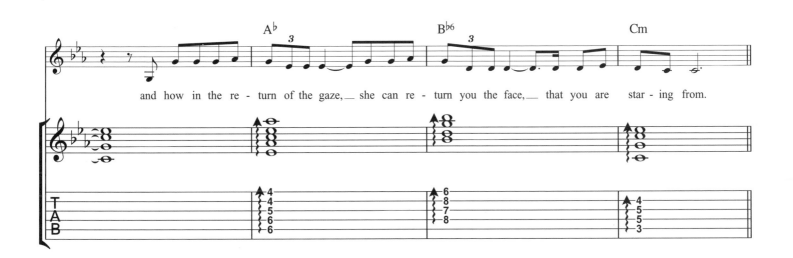

and how in the re - turn of the gaze, ___ she can re - turn you the face, ___ that you are star - ing from.

♩ = 155

Bass arr. for gtr.

(C)

Gtr 2 (elec.)

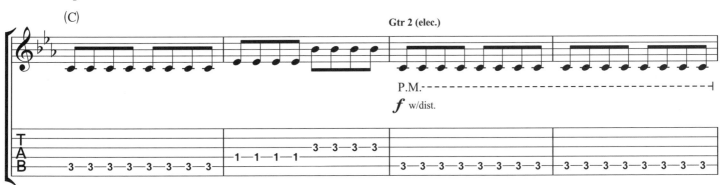

P.M. - |

f w/dist.

Gtr 3 (elec.) dbls.

*chords implied by harmony

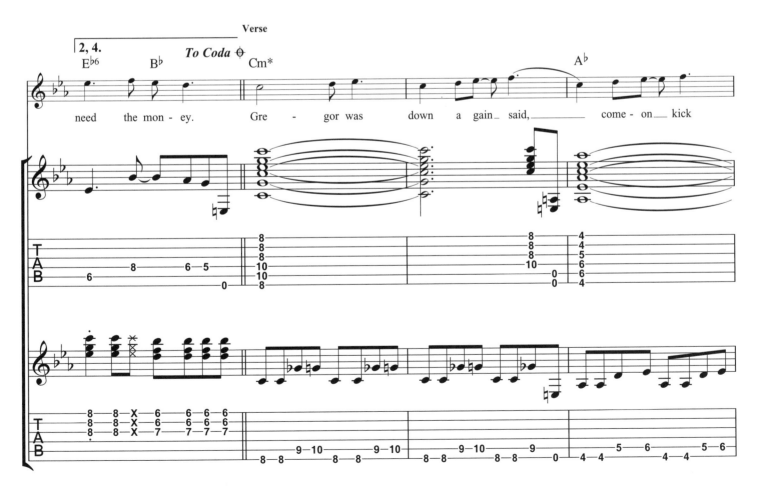

me a - gain__ said, I'm so drunk__ I don't__ mind_____ if you kill__

let ring...

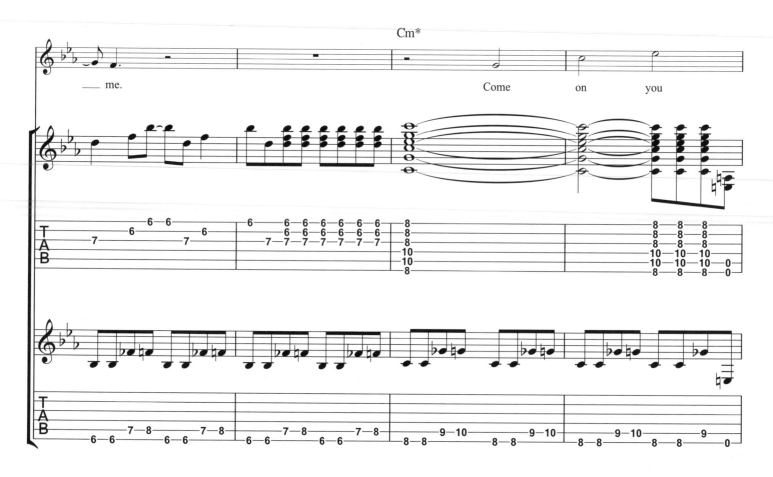

__ me.

Come on you

8

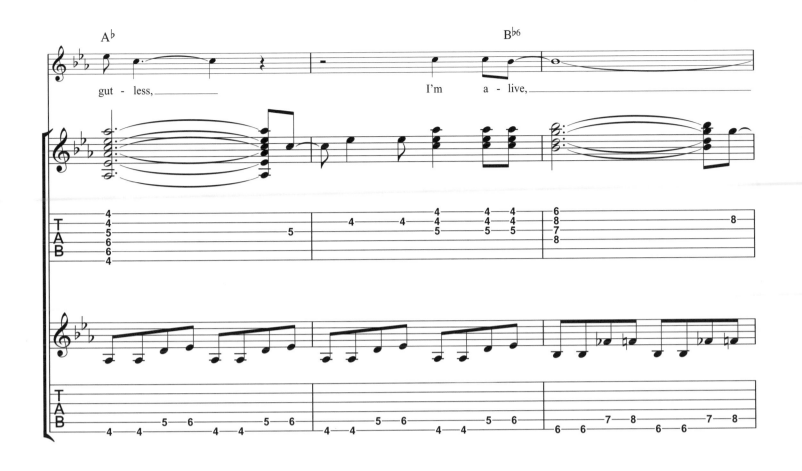

gut - less,_____ I'm a - live,_____

_____ oh, I'm a - live._____

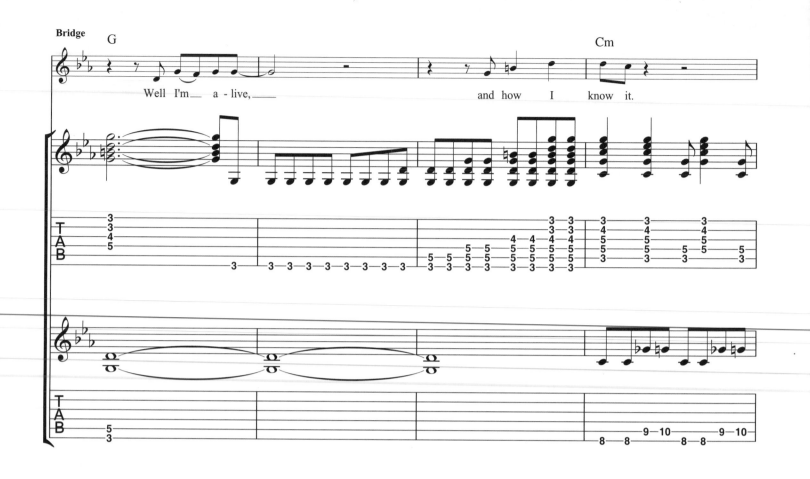

Well I'm a-live,___ and how I know it.

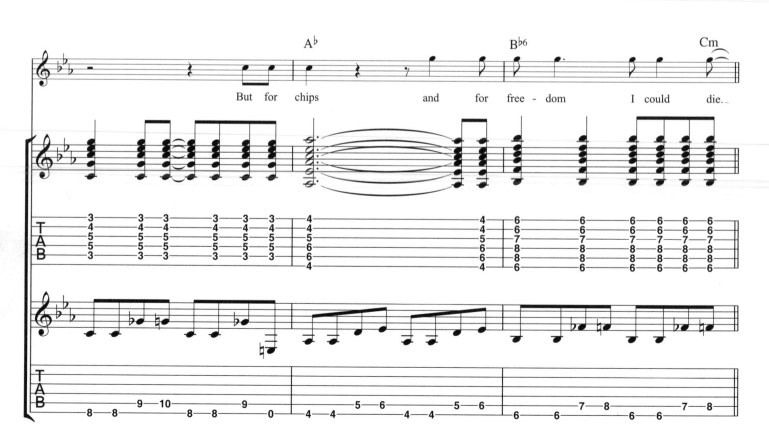

But for chips and for free-dom I could die._

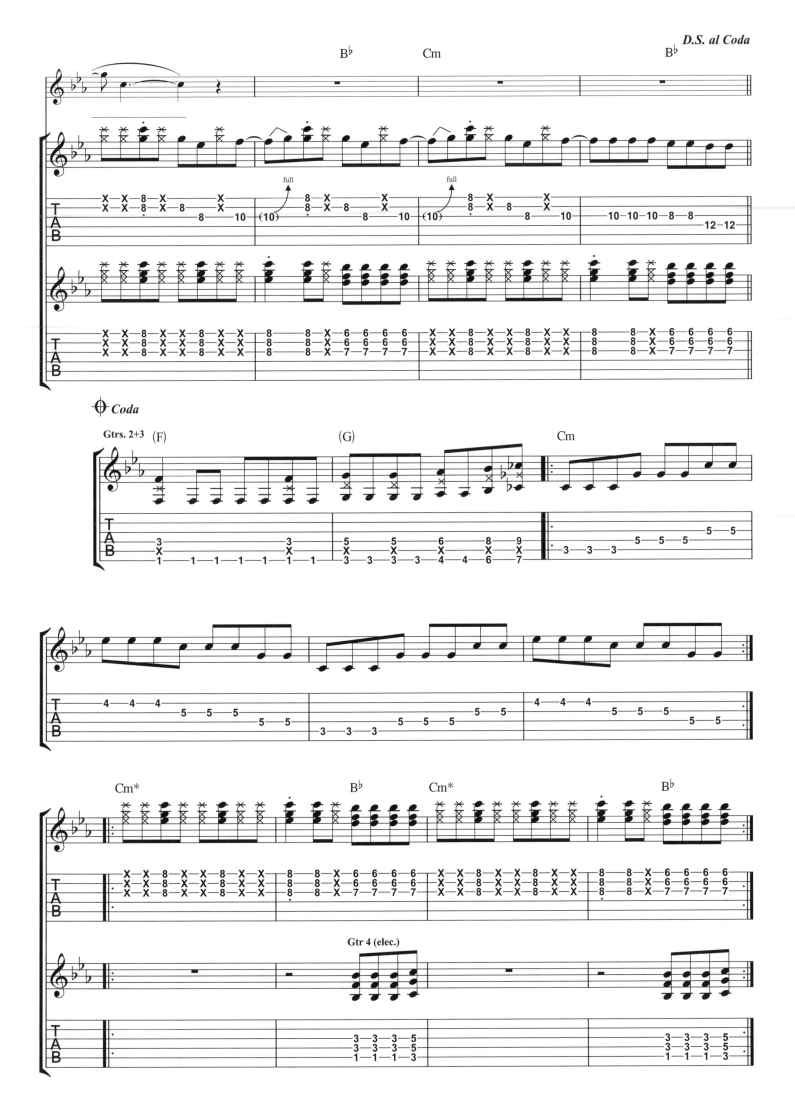

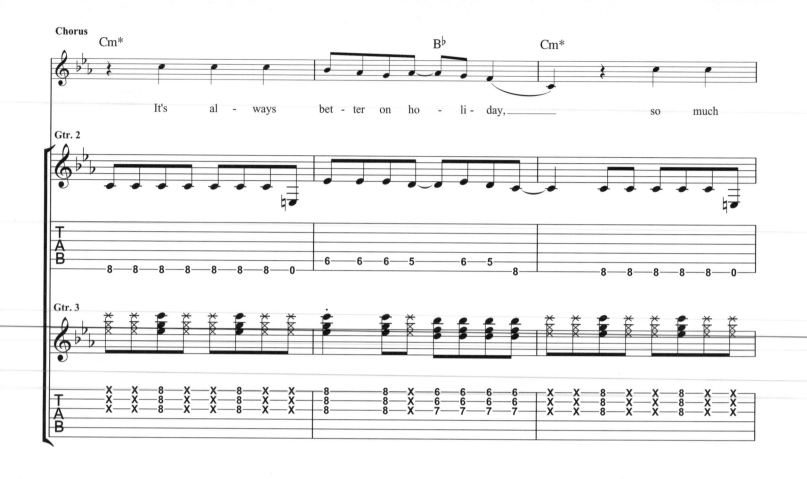

It's   al - ways   bet - ter on ho - li - day,_____   so   much

bet - ter on ho - li - day.   That's   why   we   on - ly   work_ when_____

we need the mon-ey. It's al-ways

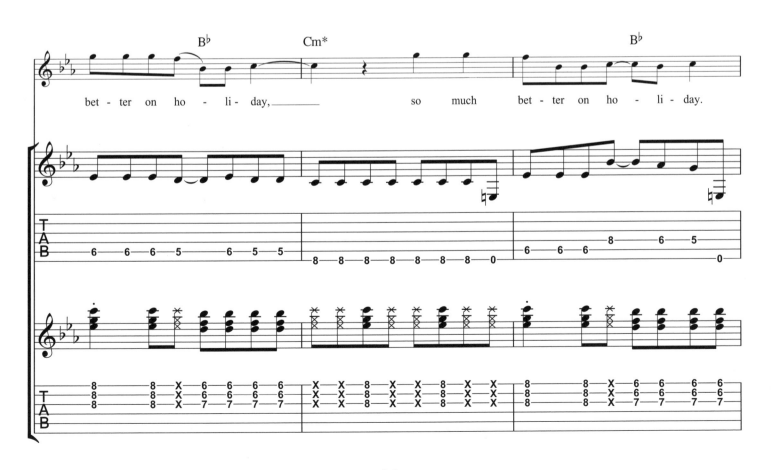

bet-ter on ho-li-day,_____ so much bet-ter on ho-li-day.

13

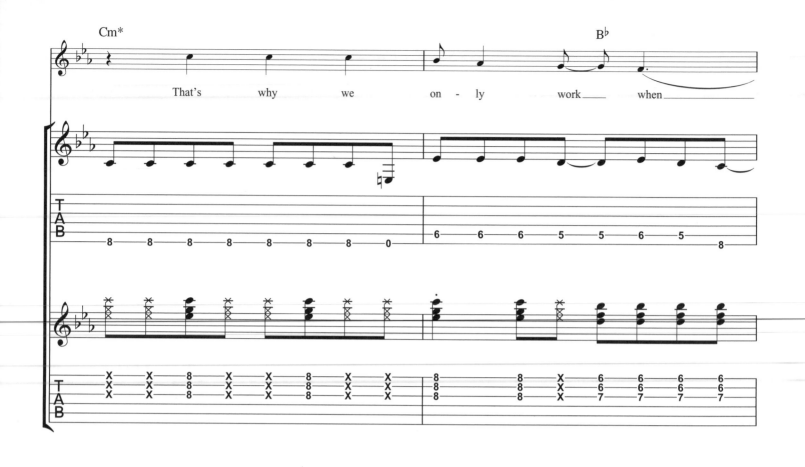

That's why we on - ly work when

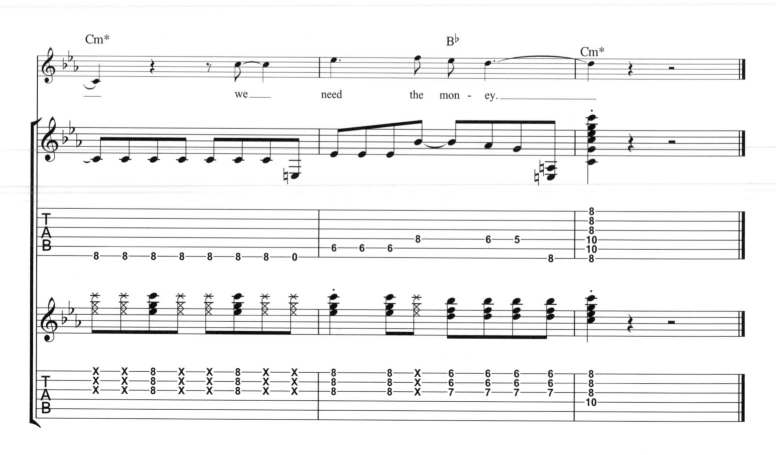

we need the mon - ey.

tell her tonight

Words & Music by Alexander Kapranos & Nicholas McCarthy

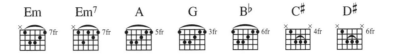

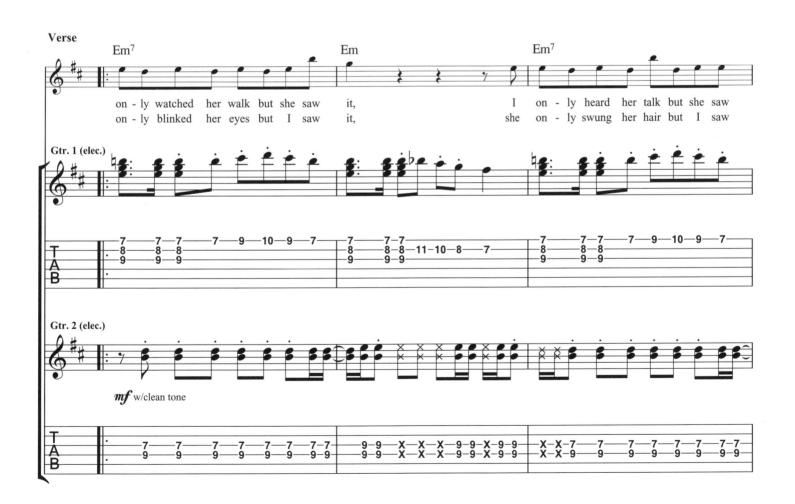

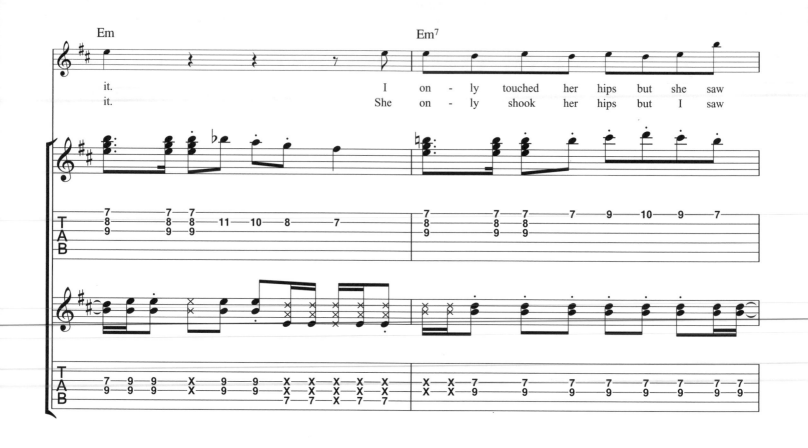

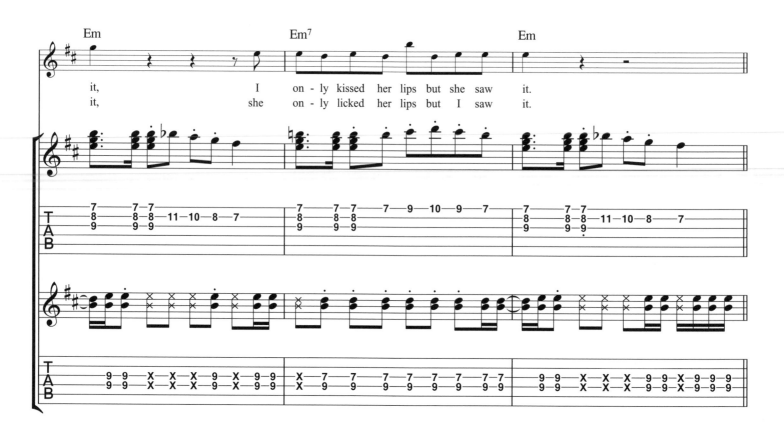

16

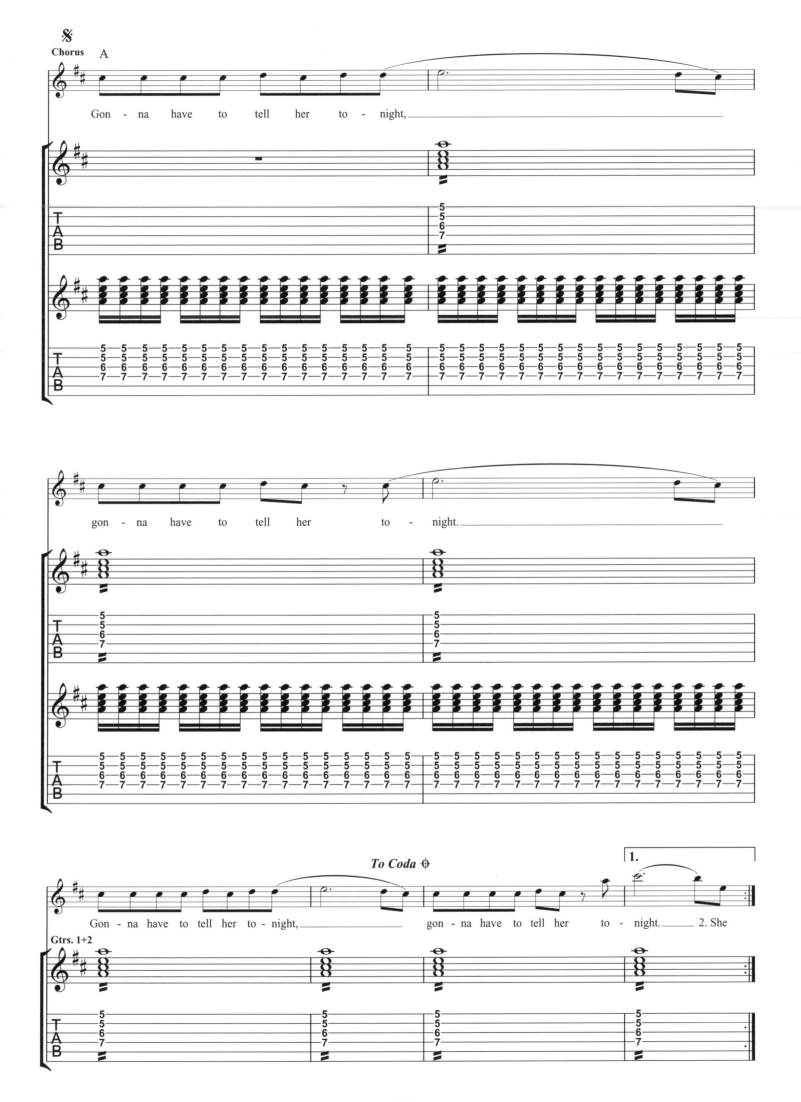

D.S. al Coda Coda

Bridge

Gtr. 2

Gtrs. 1+3

Gtr 3. w/slight dist.

take me out

Words & Music by Alexander Kapranos & Nicholas McCarthy

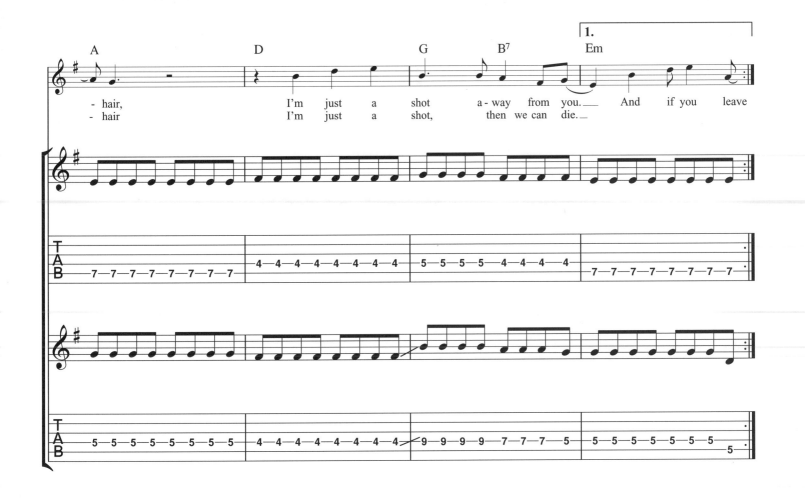

I'm just a shot a-way from you.___ And if you leave

I'm just a shot, then we can die.___

Aah,____

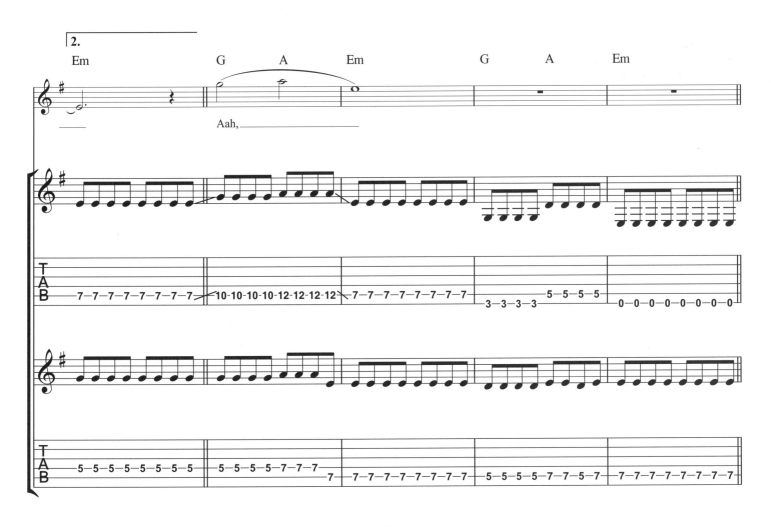

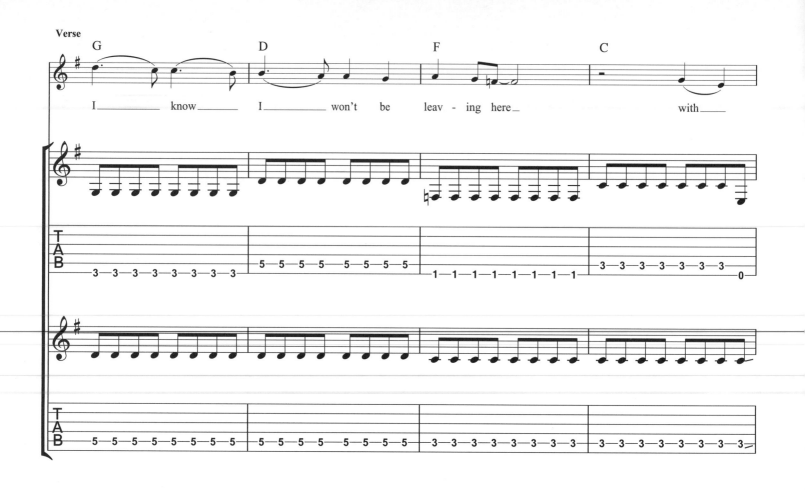

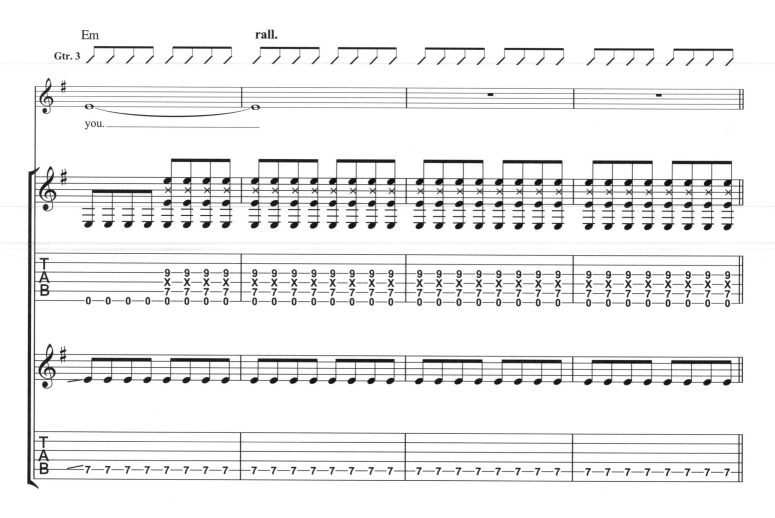

24

I say ___ you don't show, ___ don't move ___ time is slow. ___
if I move ___ things could die, ___ if eyes move, ___ this could die. ___
if I wink, this could die, if I blink, this could die. ___

I say
I want you
I want you

take me out ___ to take me out. ___

25

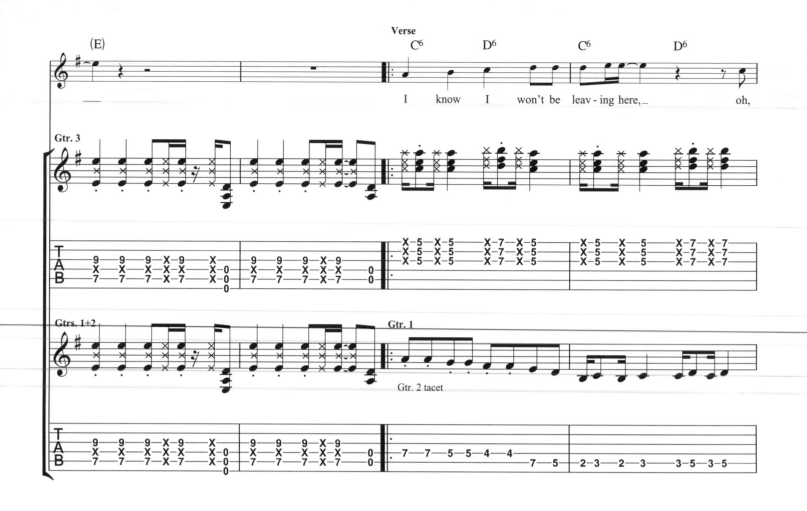

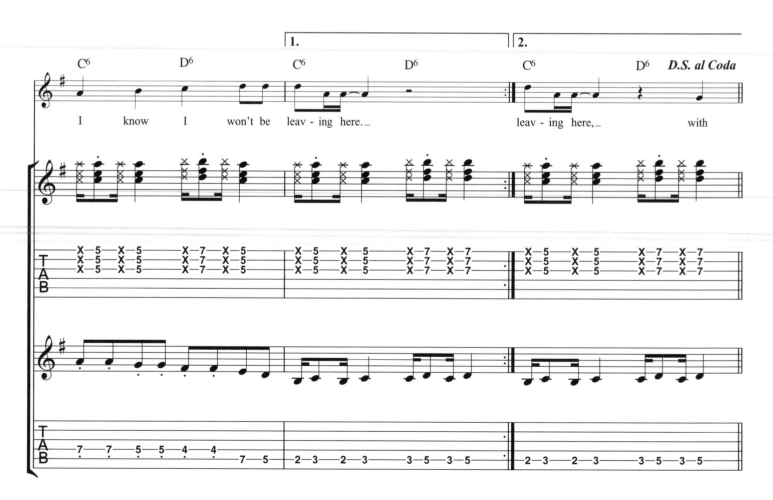

the dark of the matinée

Words & Music by Alexander Kapranos, Nicholas McCarthy & Robert Hardy

*chords implied by harmony

Gtr. 1

mf w/clean tone + tremolo

1. You take your white fin - ger,_____ slide the nail__ un - der_____ the top an bot - tom but - ton

of my bla - zer._____ Re - lax the fray - ing wool,__ slack - en ties and I'm_____

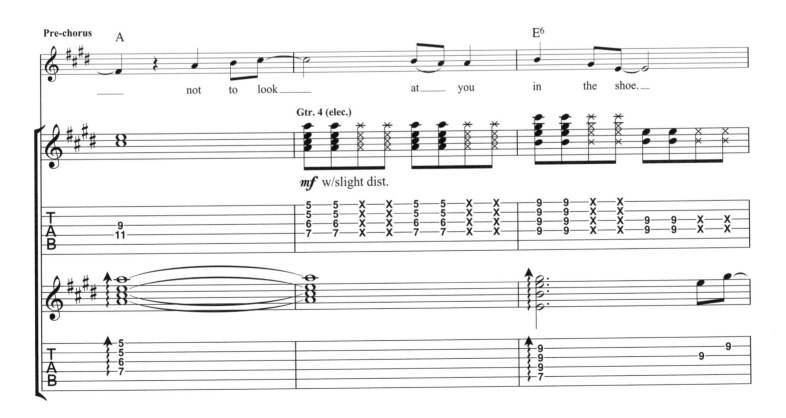

Pre-chorus

not to look_____ at__ you in the shoe._____

Gtr. 4 (elec.)

mf w/slight dist.

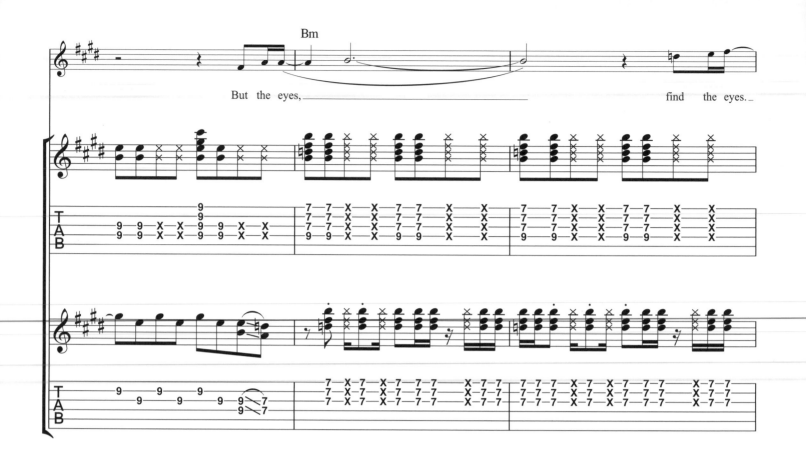

But the eyes,⎯⎯⎯⎯⎯⎯⎯⎯⎯⎯⎯⎯⎯⎯⎯⎯⎯⎯⎯ find the eyes.

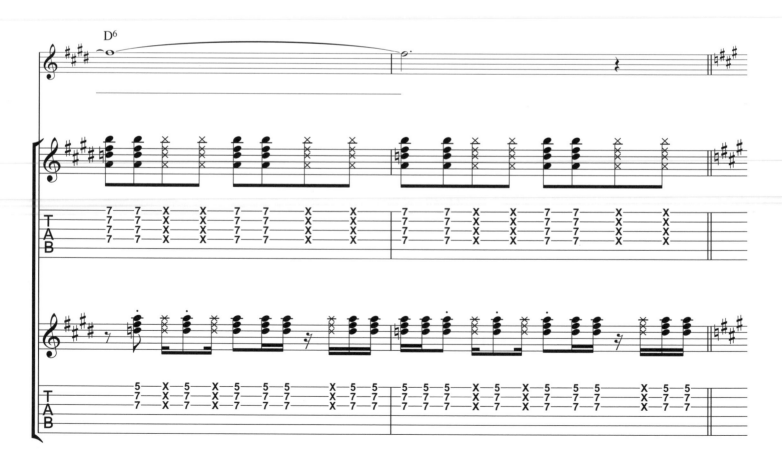

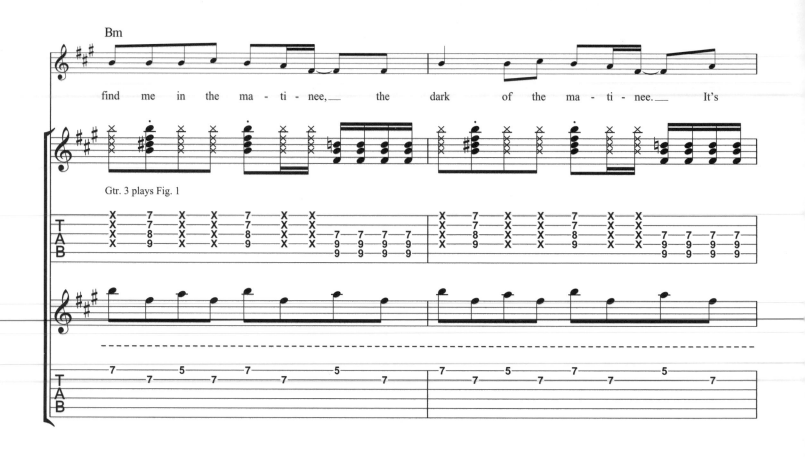

find me in the ma-ti-nee,___ the dark of the ma-ti-nee.___ It's

Gtr. 3 plays Fig. 1

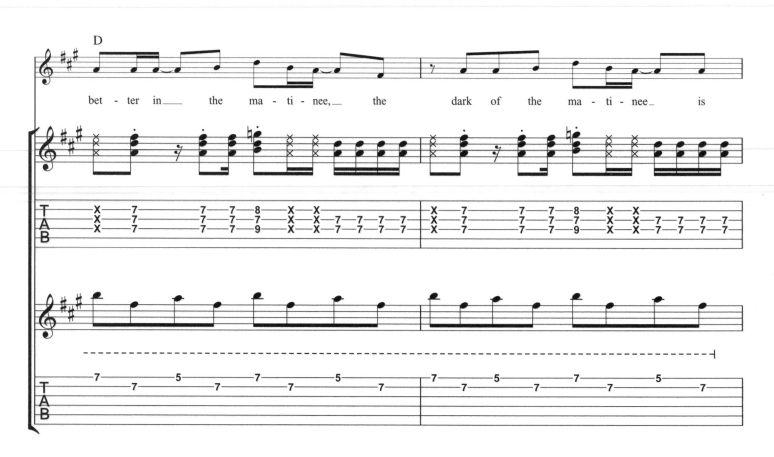

bet-ter in___ the ma-ti-nee,___ the dark of the ma-ti-nee___ is

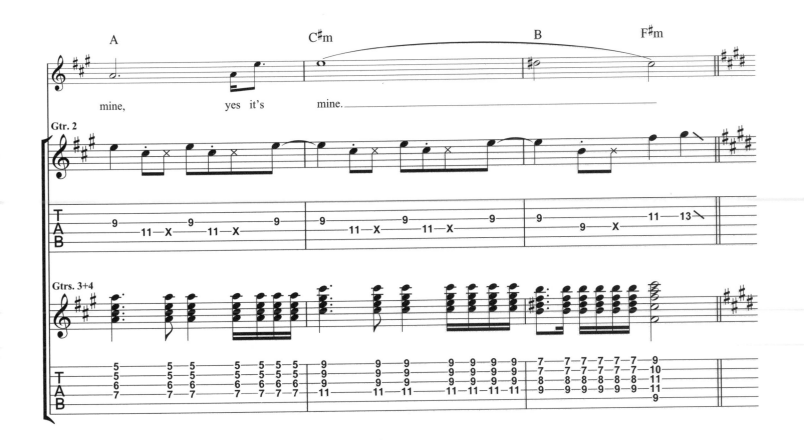

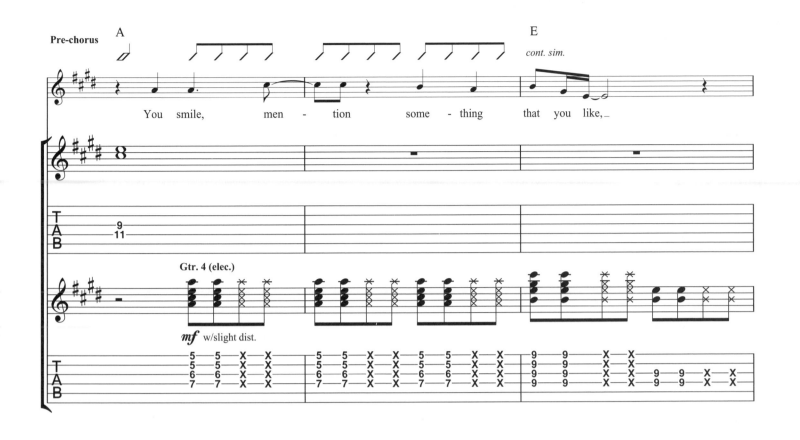

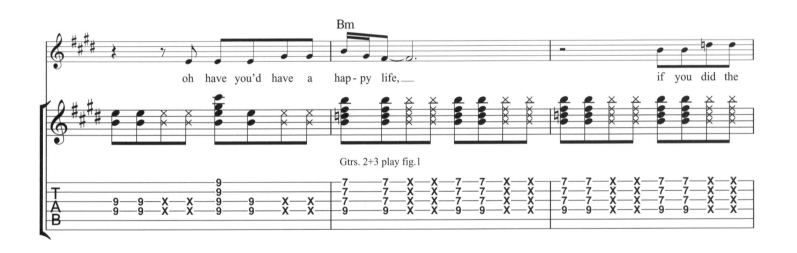

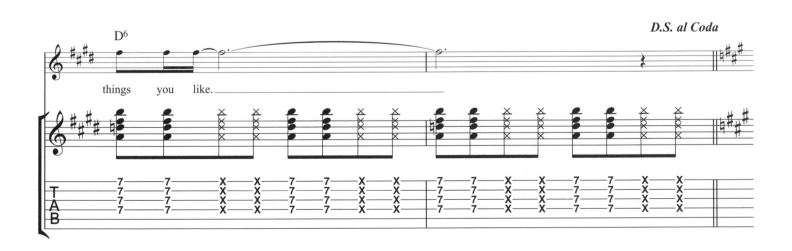

My words and smile_____ are so ea-sy now,_____ Yes it's

Gtr. 3

♩ = 114

Bm

ea - sy now,___ yes it's

Gtrs. 2+3

D

ea - sy now._____

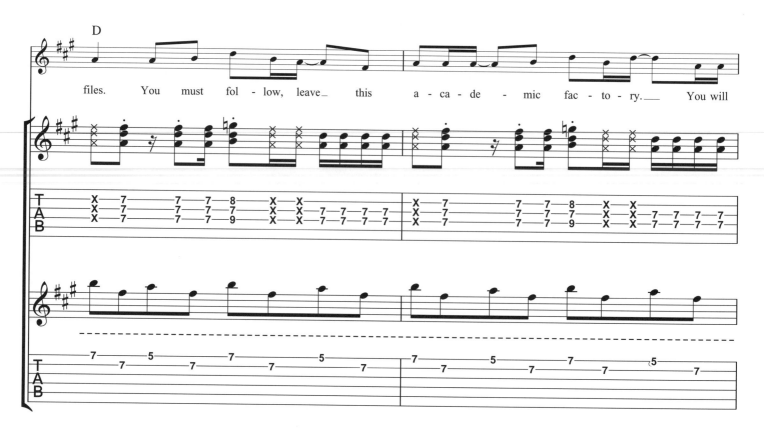

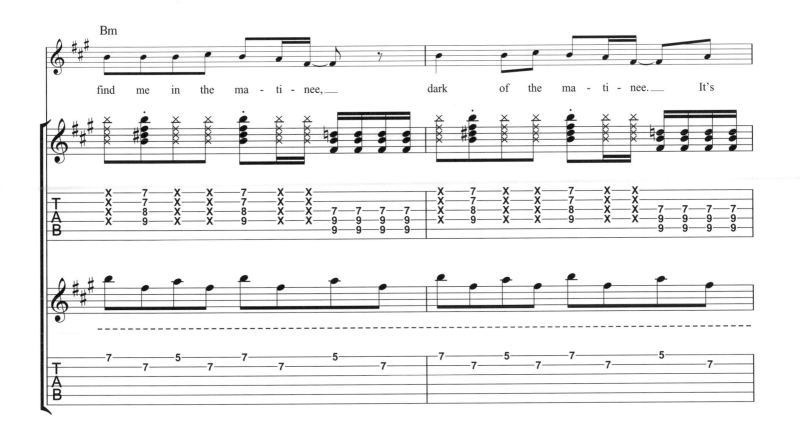

find me in the ma-ti-nee,___ dark of the ma-ti-nee.___ It's

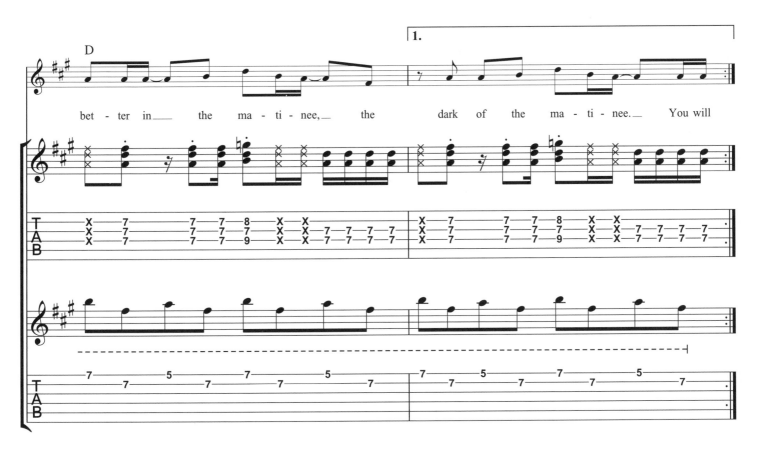

bet-ter in___ the ma-ti-nee,___ the dark of the ma-ti-nee.___ You will

dark of the ma - ti - nee___ is mine, yes it's

mine.___

auf achse

Words & Music by Alexander Kapranos & Nicholas McCarthy

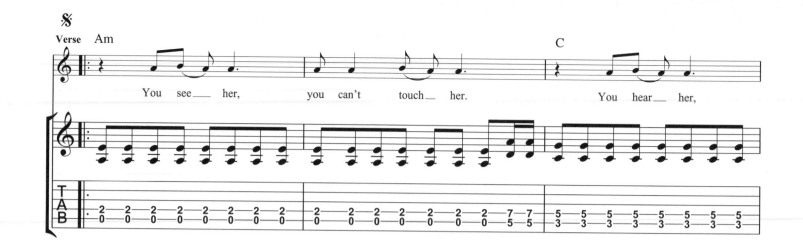

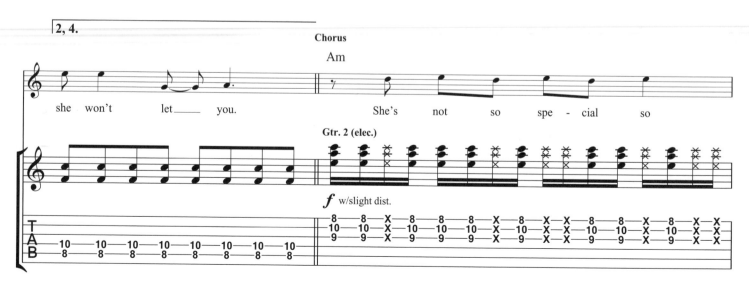

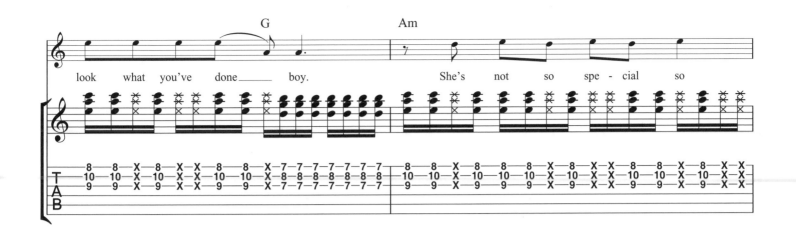

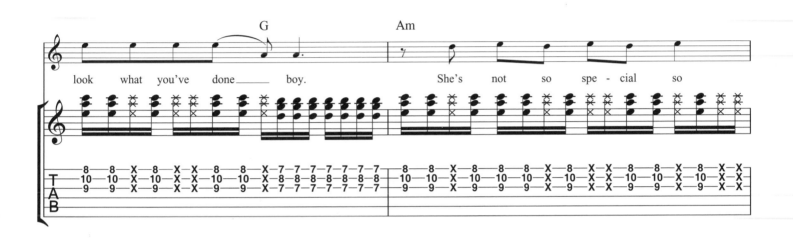

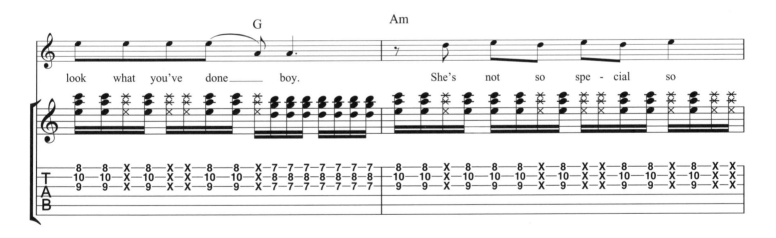

To Coda ⊕

Bridge

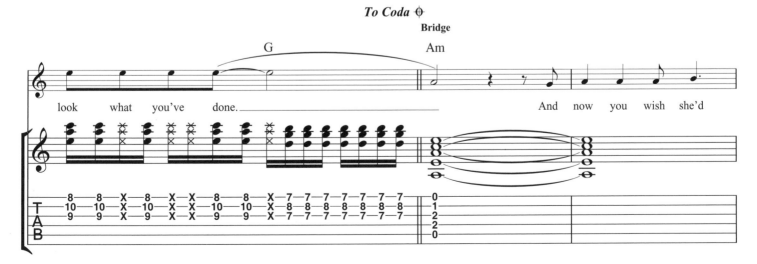

45

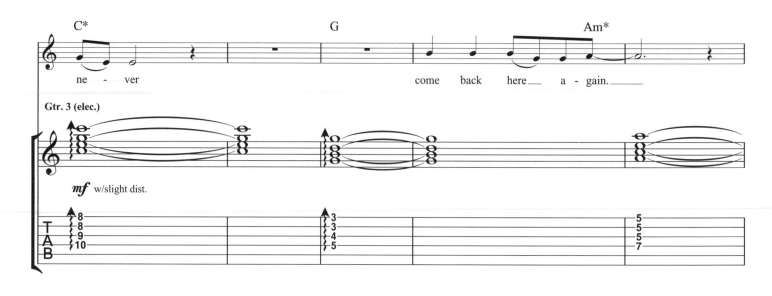

ne - ver come back here a - gain.

Gtr. 3 (elec.)

mf w/slight dist.

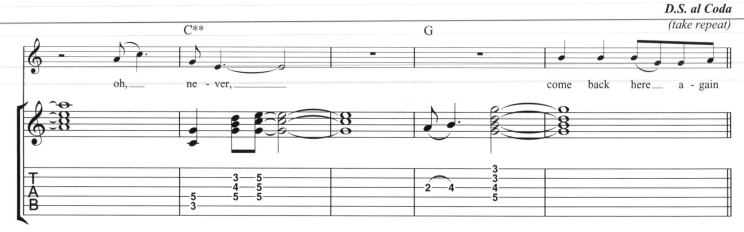

D.S. al Coda
(take repeat)

oh, ne - ver, come back here a - gain

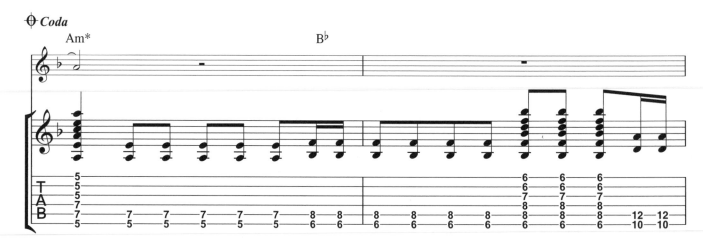

Coda

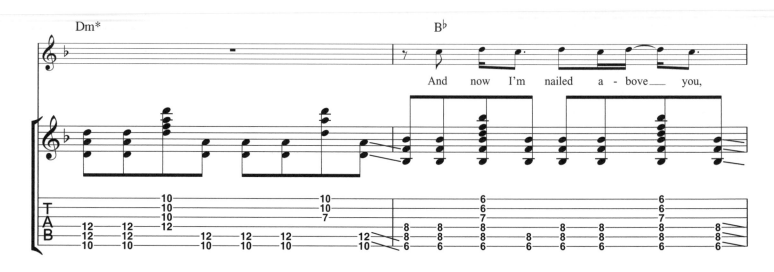

And now I'm nailed a - bove you,

46

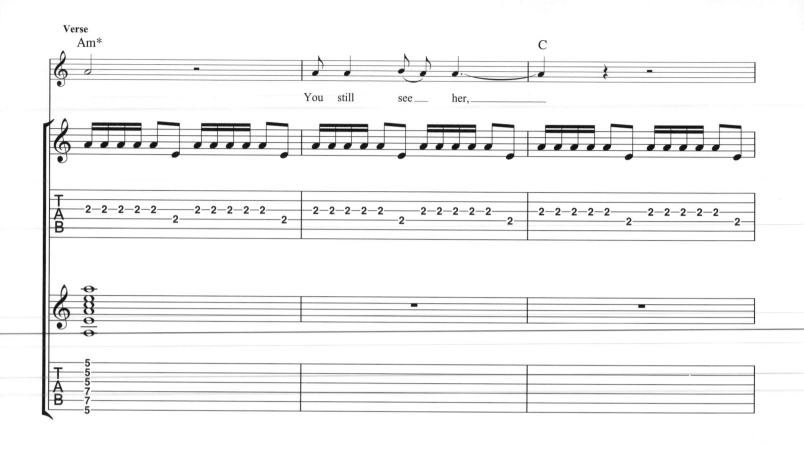

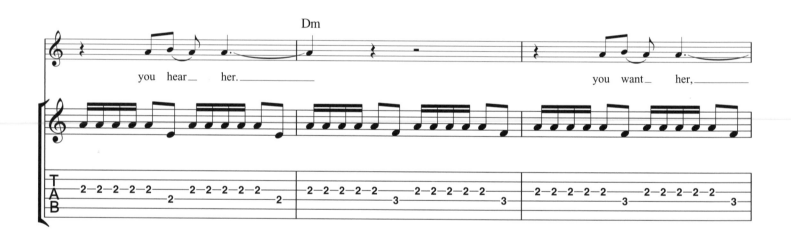

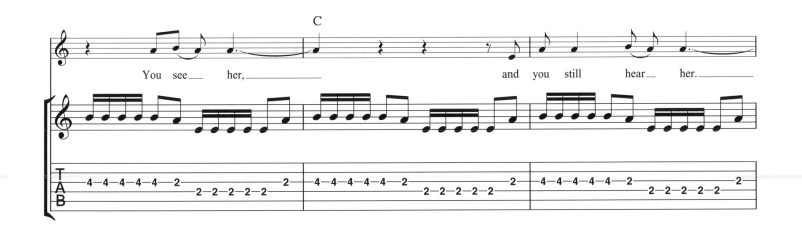

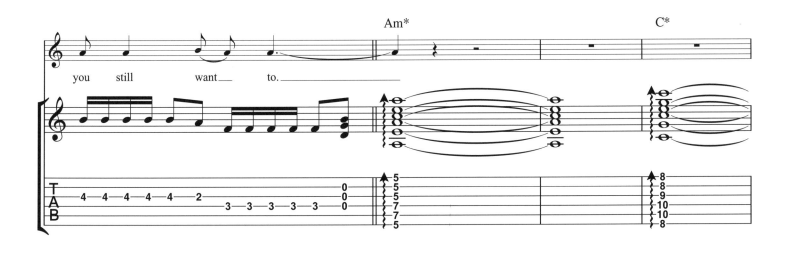

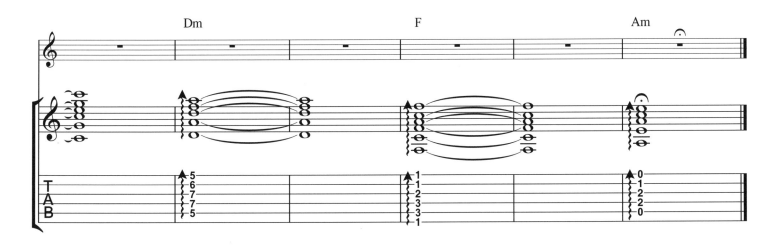

this fire

Words & Music by Alexander Kapranos & Nicholas McCarthy

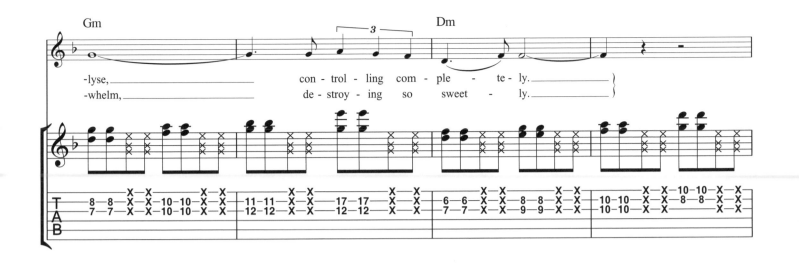

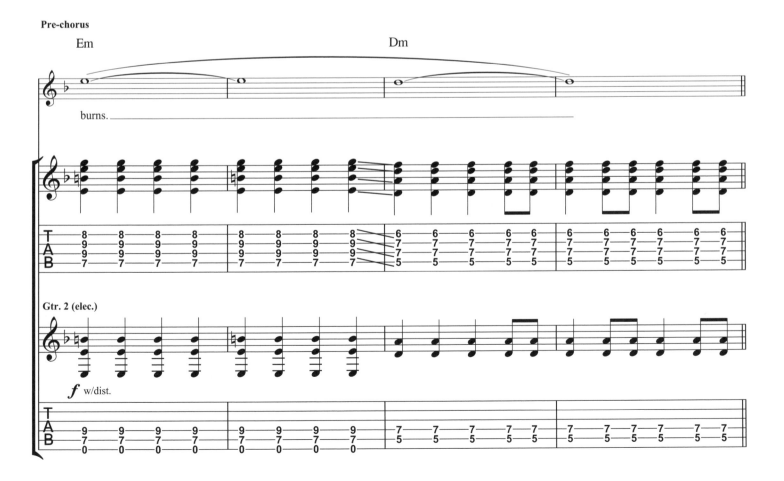

51

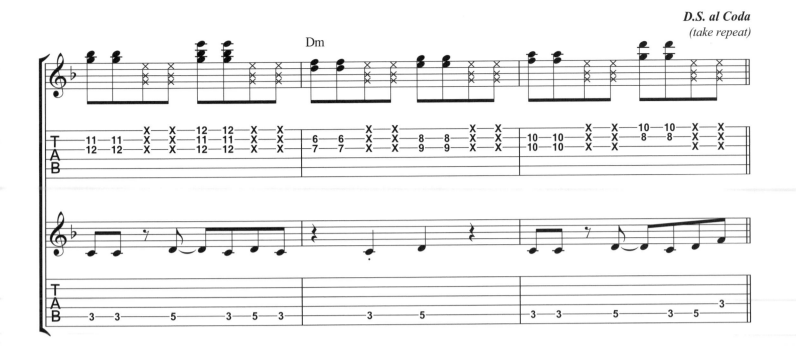

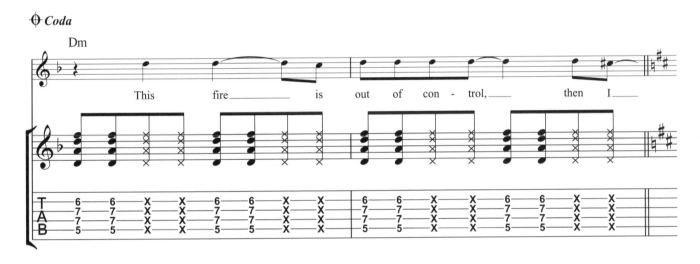

This fire___ is out of con - trol,___ then I___

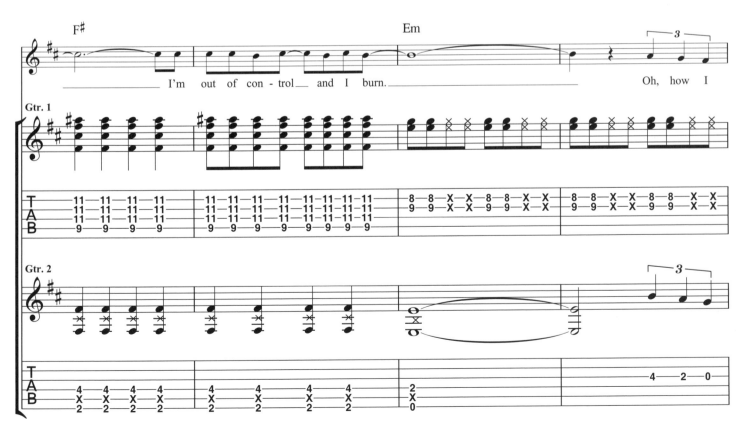

___ I'm out of con - trol___ and I burn.___ Oh, how I

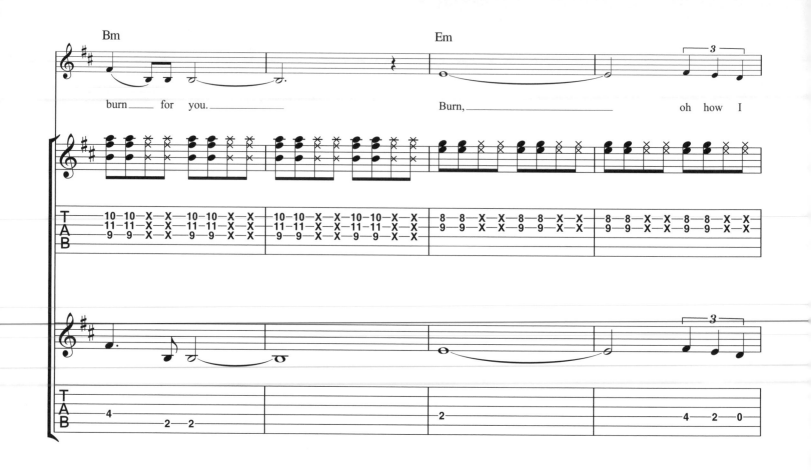

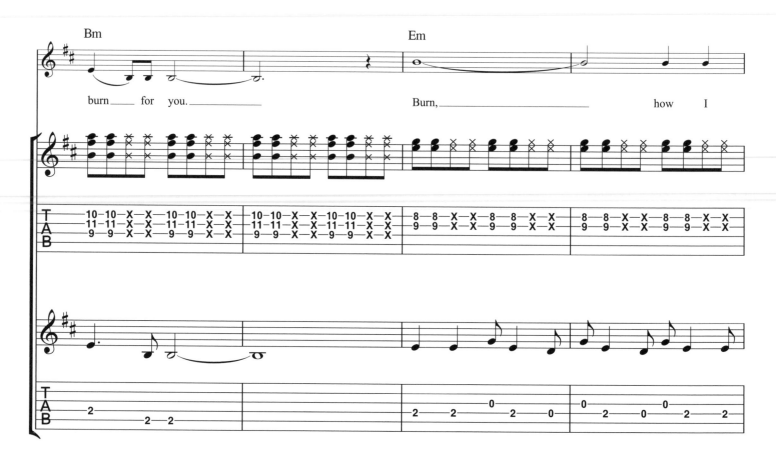

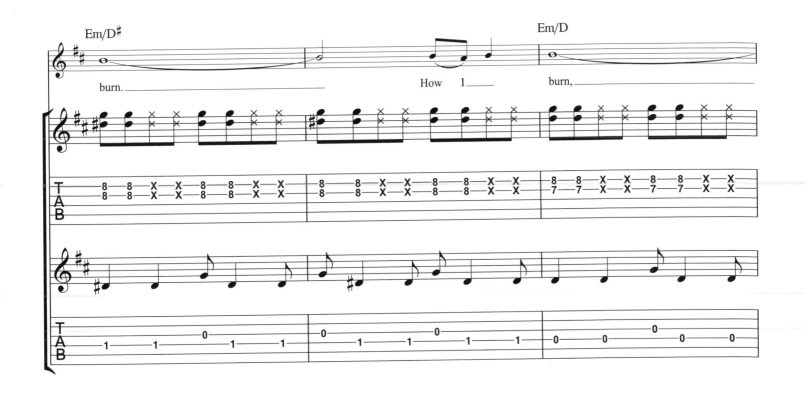

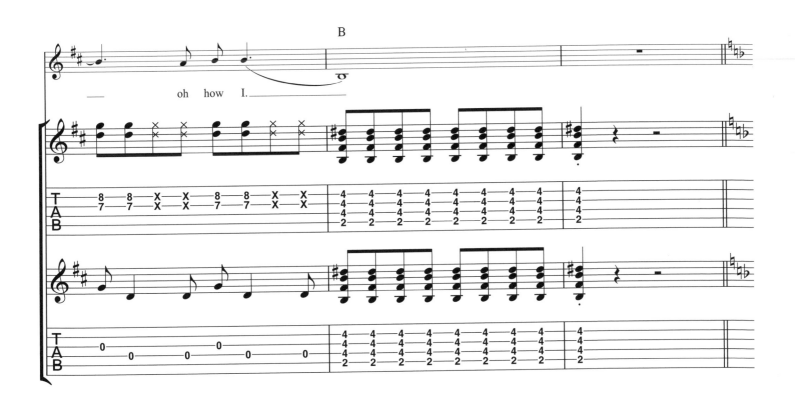

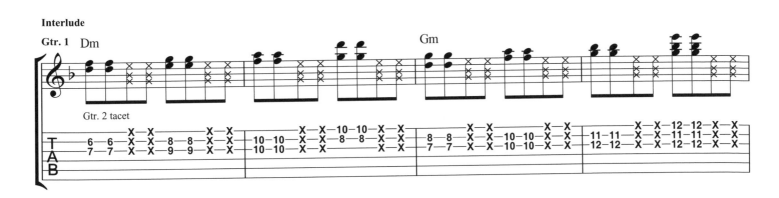

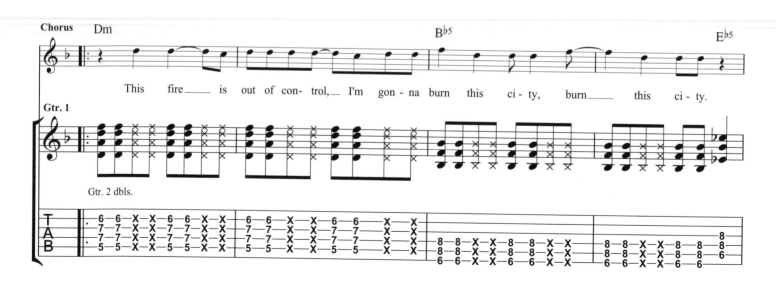

56

This fire___ is out of con-trol,___ I'm gon-na burn this ci-ty, burn___

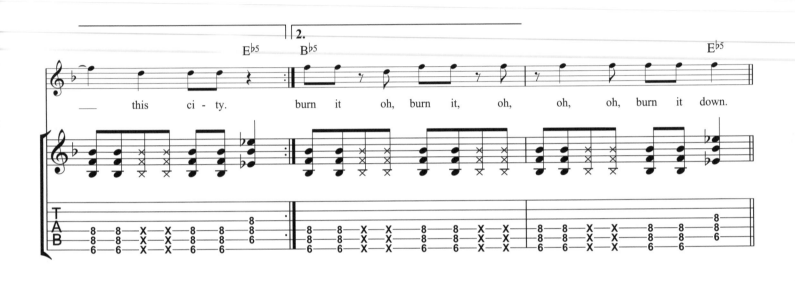

___ this ci-ty. burn it oh, burn it, oh, oh, oh, burn it down.

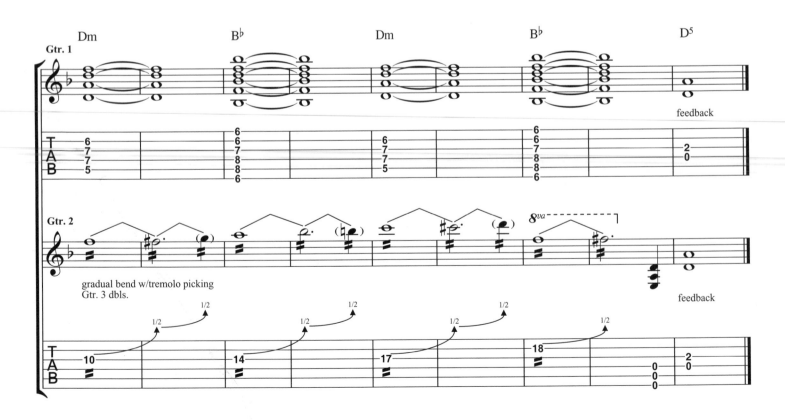

gradual bend w/tremolo picking
Gtr. 3 dbls.

feedback

darts of pleasure

Words & Music by Alexander Kapranos & Nicholas McCarthy

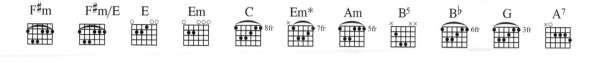

Verse

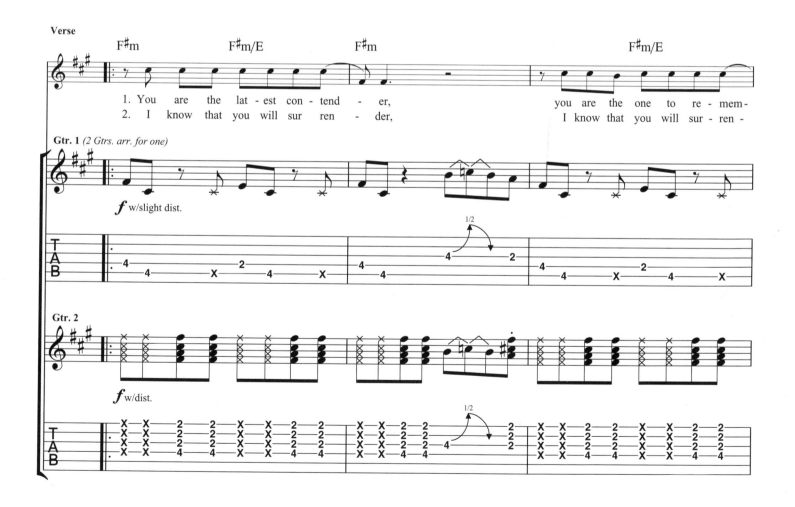

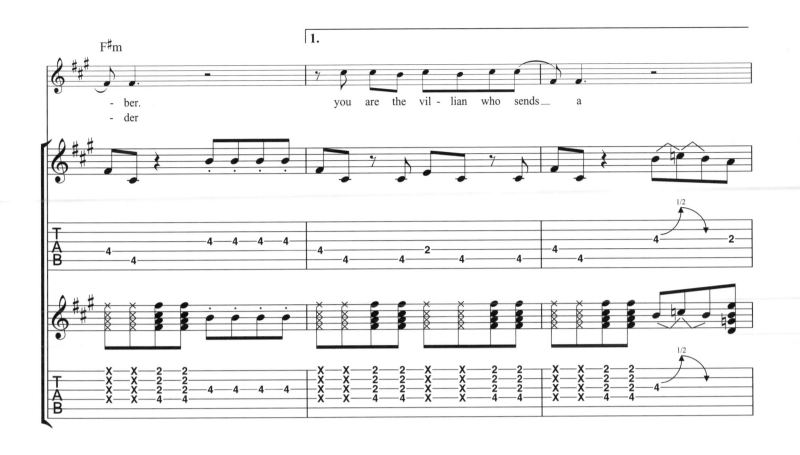

ber. / der ... you are the vil - lian who sends___ a

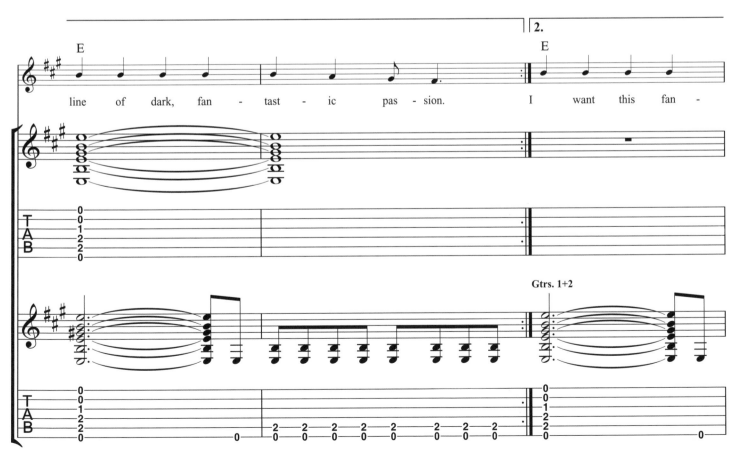

line of dark, fan - tast - ic pas - sion. I want this fan -

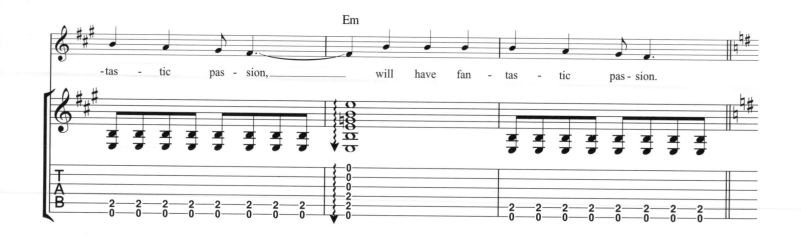

-tas - tic pas - sion,_____ will have fan - tas - tic pas - sion.

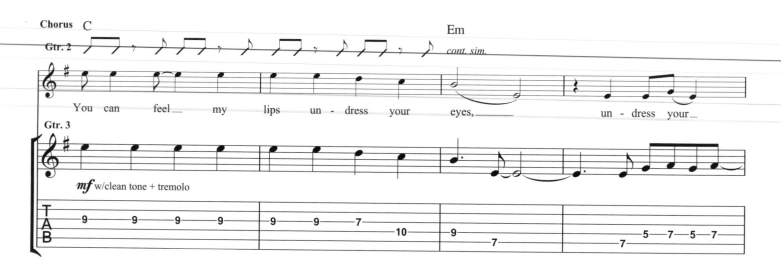

Chorus C

Gtr. 2   Em   *cont. sim.*

You can feel_ my lips un - dress your eyes,_____ un - dress your_

Gtr. 3

mf w/clean tone + tremolo

Am   Em*

eyes,   un - dress your eyes._____

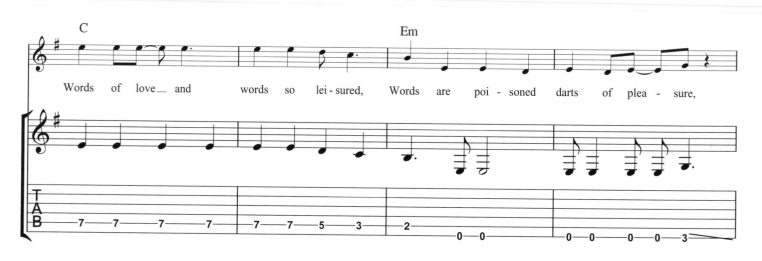

C   Em

Words of love_ and words so lei - sured, Words are poi - soned darts of plea - sure,

die,_____ and so you die._____

3. You are the lat - est ad - vent - ure,
4. I know that you will sur - ren - der, I____

Verse

Gtr. 1 *(2 Gtrs. arr. for one)*

Gtr. 2

f w/dist.

you're an e - mo - tion a - veng - er, you are the dev - il that sells___
_____ know that you will sur - ren - der

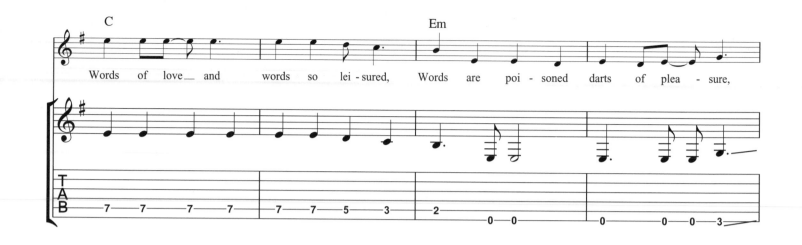

Words of love__ and words so lei-sured, Words are poi-soned darts of plea-sure,

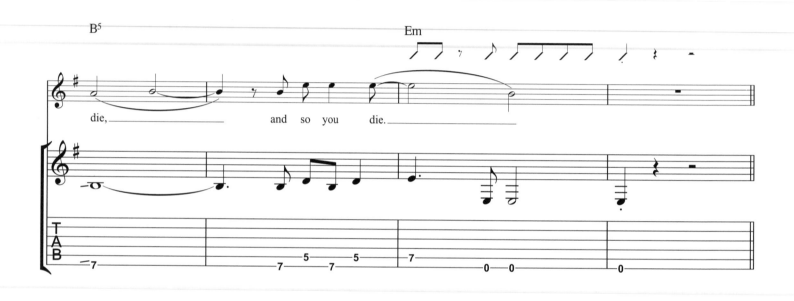

die,_____ and so you die._____

Interlude

Bass arr. for gtr

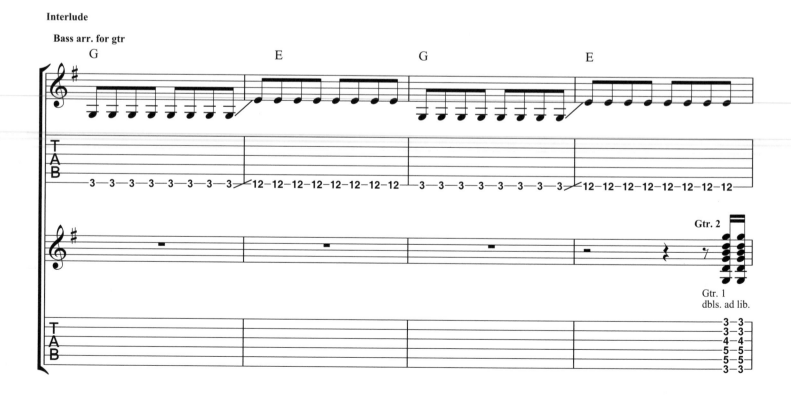

Gtr. 2

Gtr. 1
dbls. ad lib.

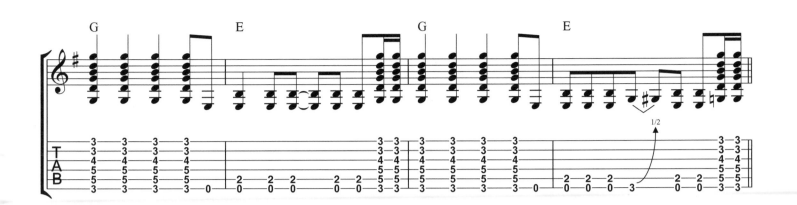

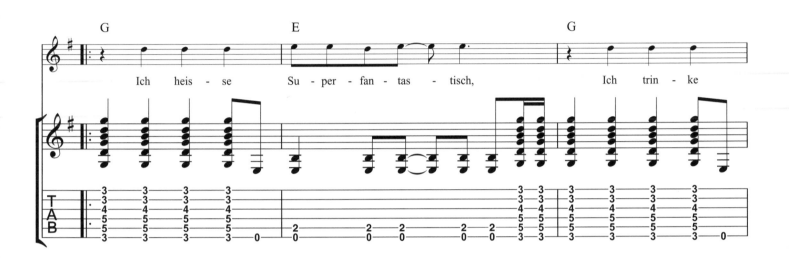

Ich heis - se Su - per - fan - tas - tisch, Ich trin - ke

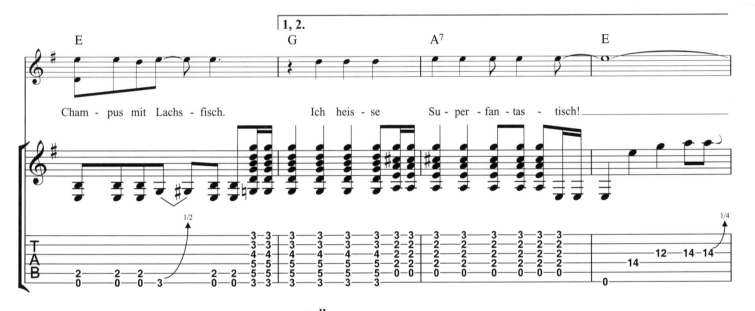

1, 2.

Cham - pus mit Lachs - fisch. Ich heis - se Su - per - fan - tas - tisch!

rall.

3.

Su - per - fan - tas - tische!

65

cheating on you

Words & Music by Alexander Kapranos & Nicholas McCarthy

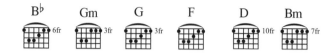

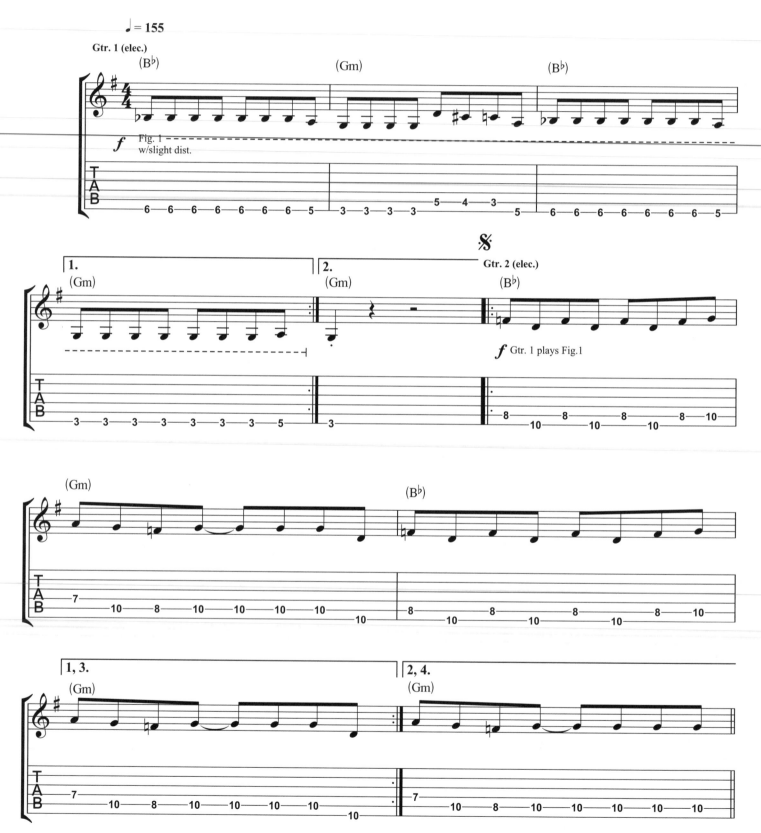

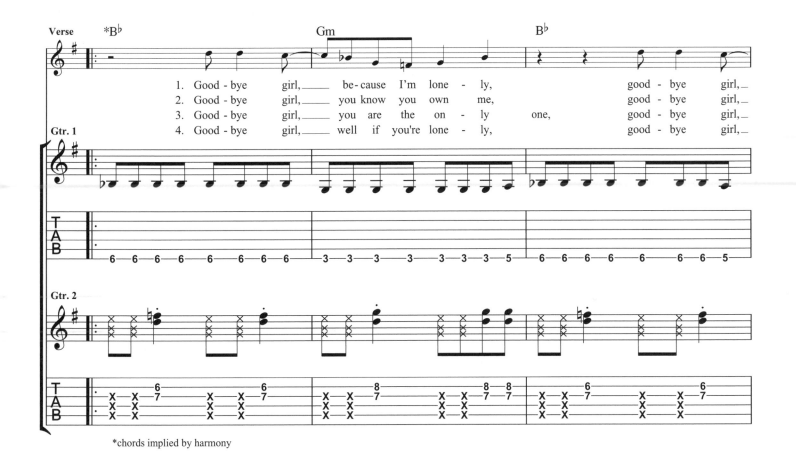

*chords implied by harmony

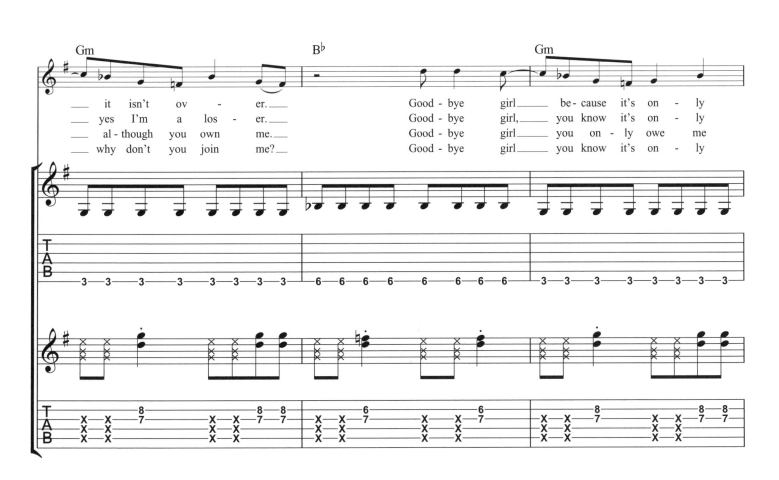

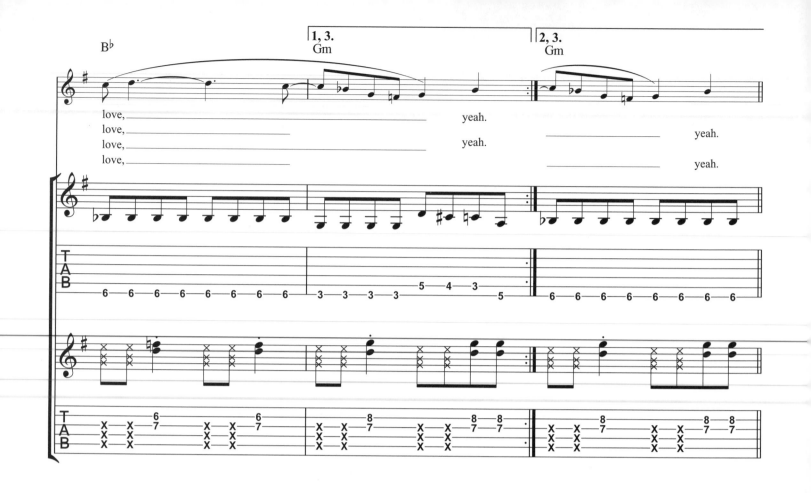

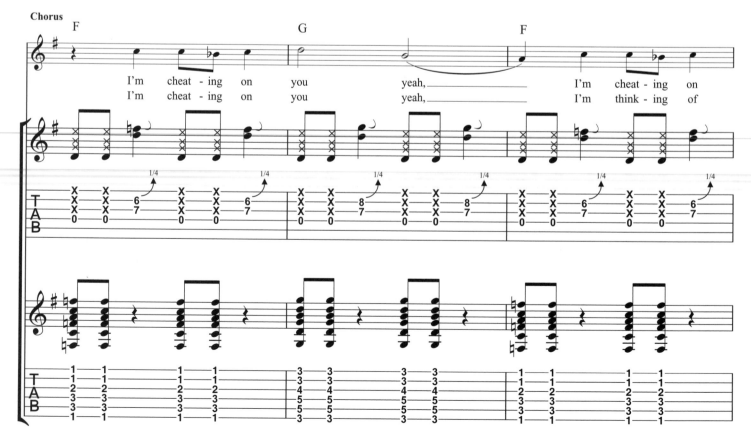

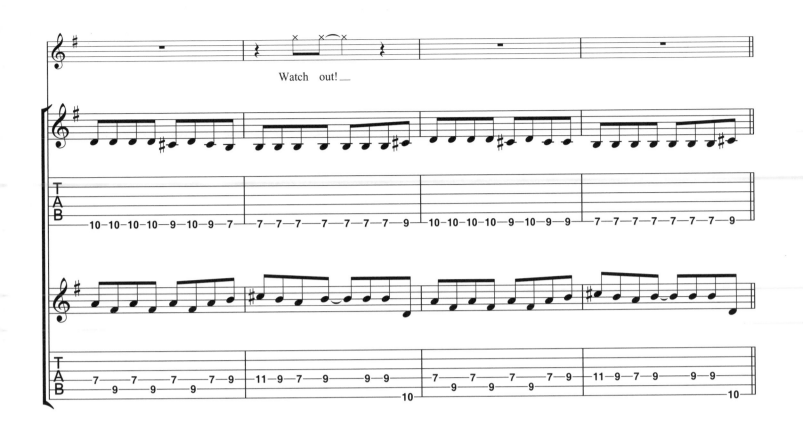

Watch out! ___

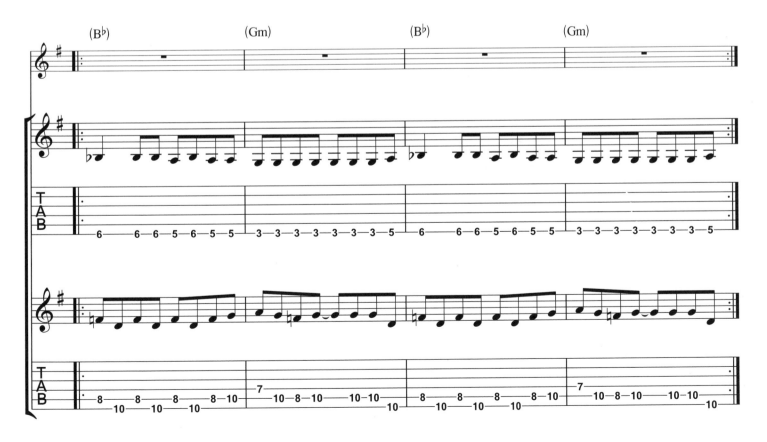

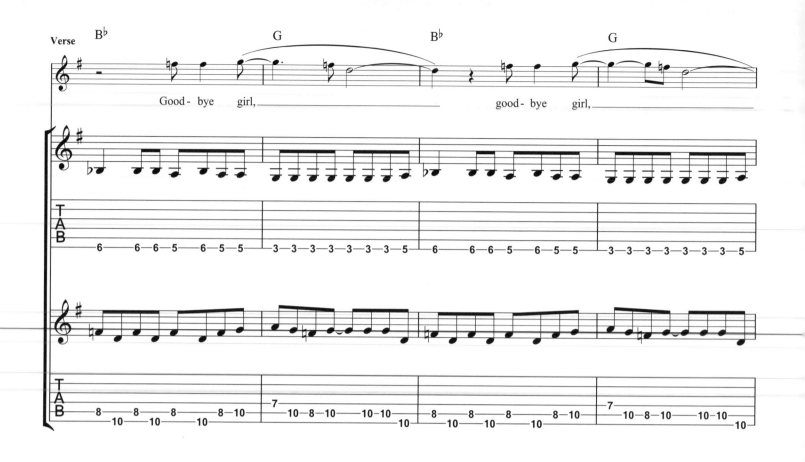

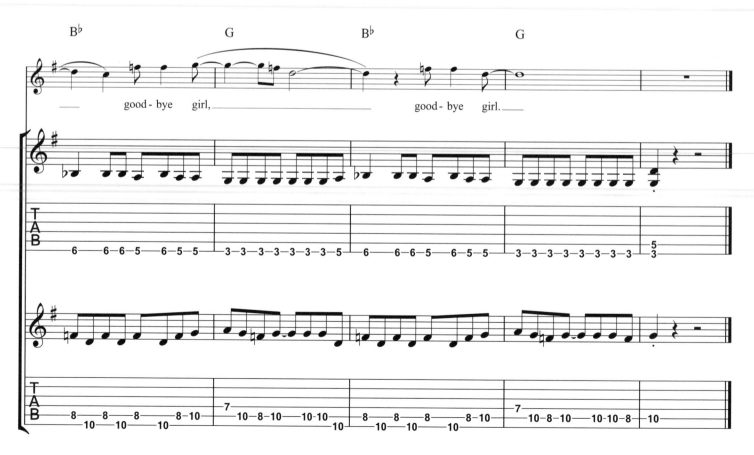

michael

Words & Music by Alexander Kapranos & Nicholas McCarthy

1. This is where I'll be___ so hea - ven - ly,___ so come and dance with me Mi - chael.
2. This is what I am,___ I am a man,___ so come and dance with me Mi - chael.

So se - xy, I'm se - xy,___ so come and dance with me Mi - chael.
So strong now, it's strong now,___ so come and dance with me Mi - chael.

I'm all that you see,___ you wan-na see,___ so come and dance with me Mi - chael.

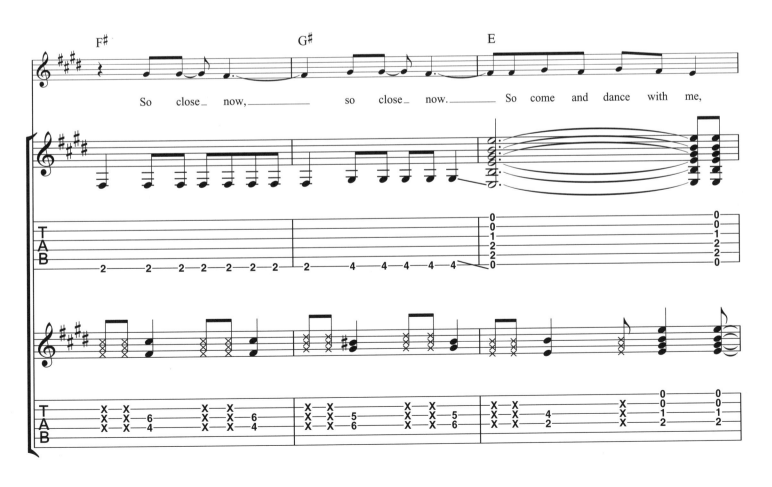

So close___ now,_____ so close___ now.___ So come and dance with me,

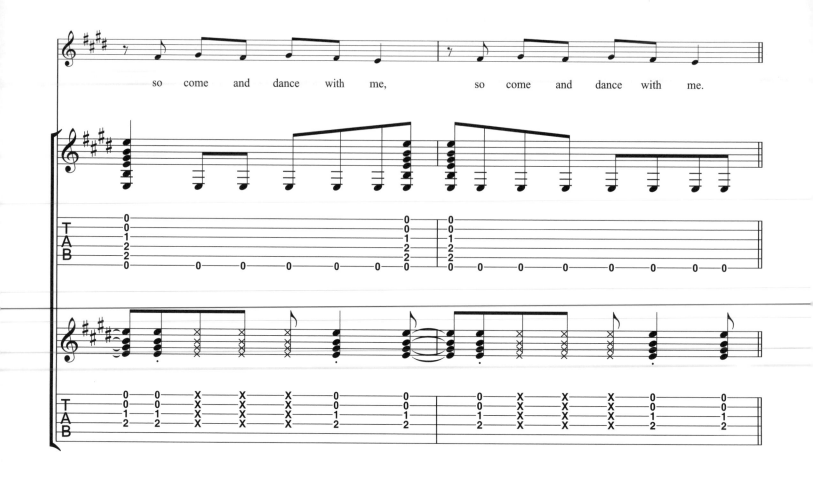

so come and dance with me, so come and dance with me.

Chorus

C#   A   F#

1. 2. Mi - chael, you're the boy___ with all the lea - ther hips, stick - y hair, stick - y hips, stub-
3. Mi - chael you're the on - ly one I'd ev - er want, on - ly one I'd ev - er want, on -

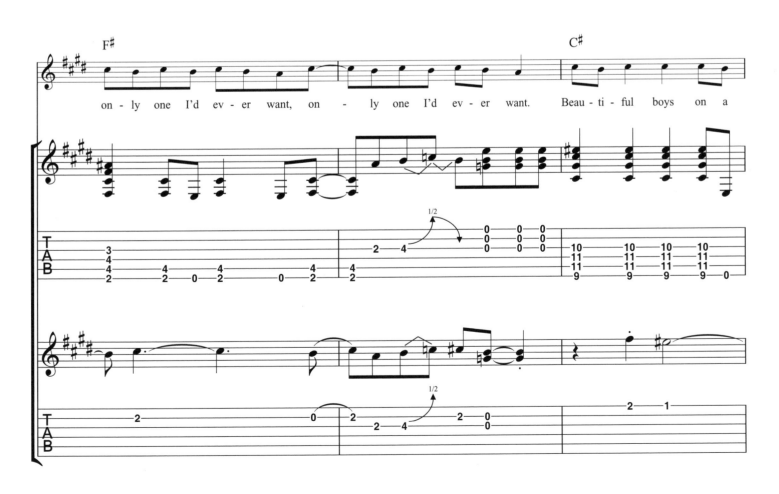

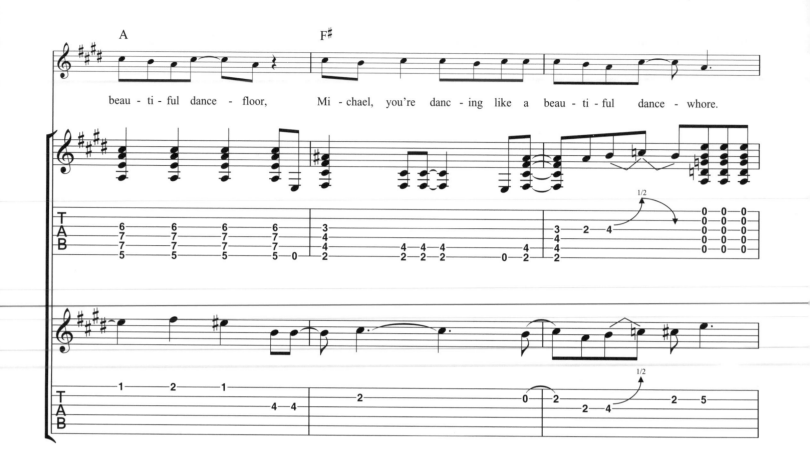

beau - ti - ful dance - floor, Mi - chael, you're danc - ing like a beau - ti - ful dance - whore.

Mi - chael wait - ing on a silv - er plat - ter now,_____ and no - thing mat - ters now.

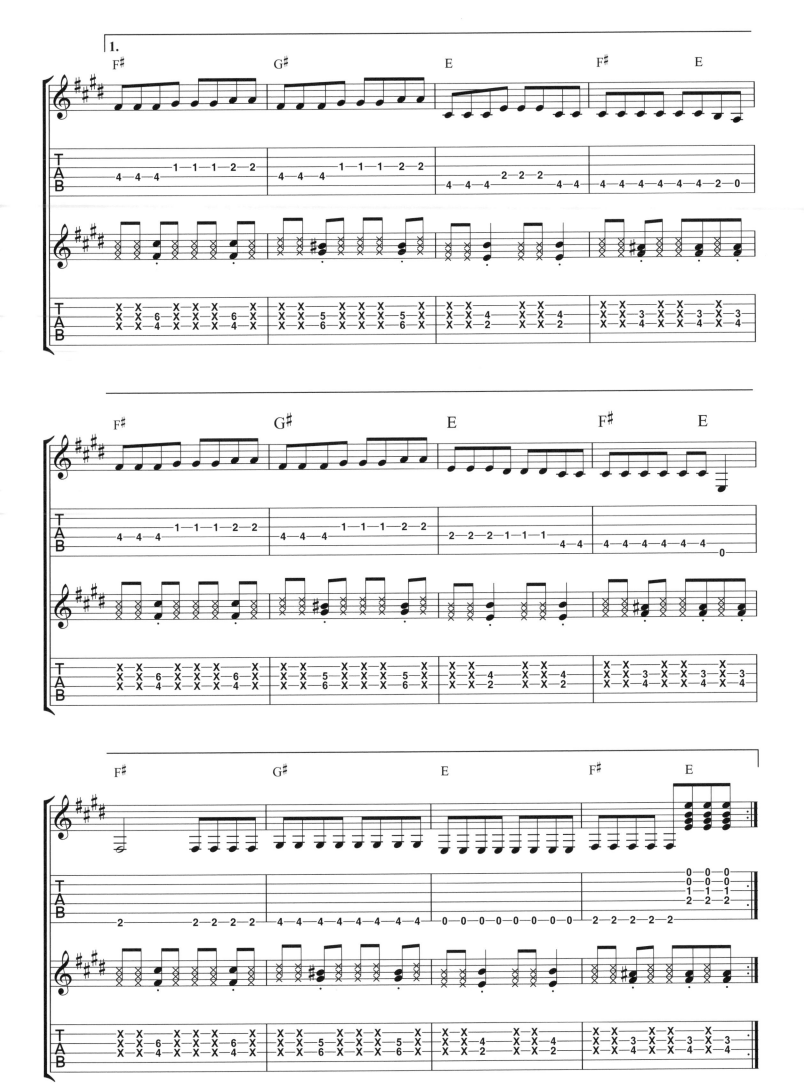

silver plat-ter now, no-thing mat-ters now,

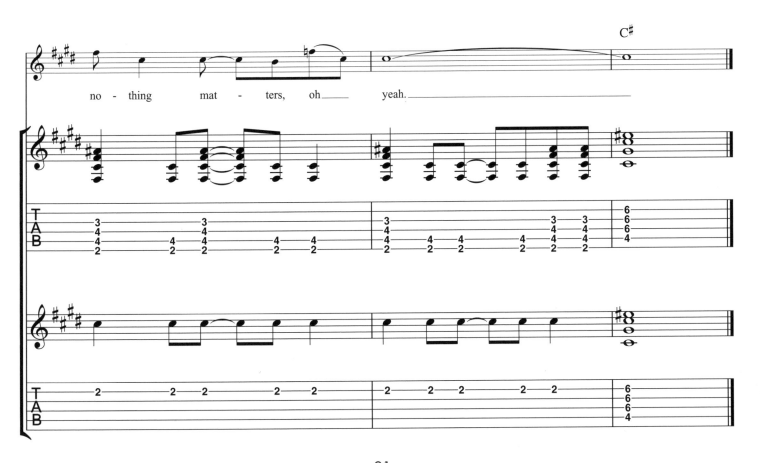

no-thing mat-ters, oh_____ yeah._____

come on home

Words & Music by Alexander Kapranos & Nicholas McCarthy

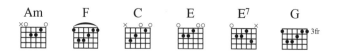

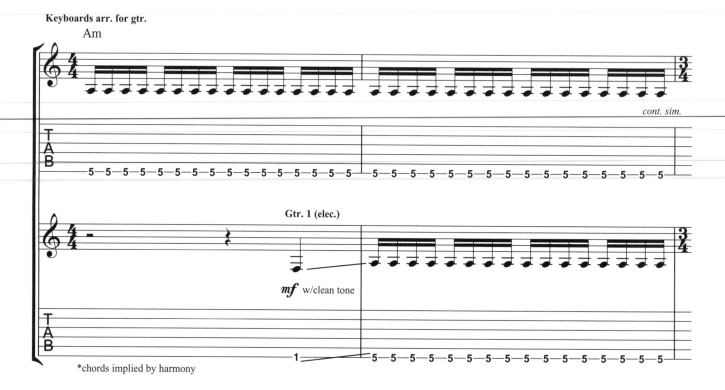

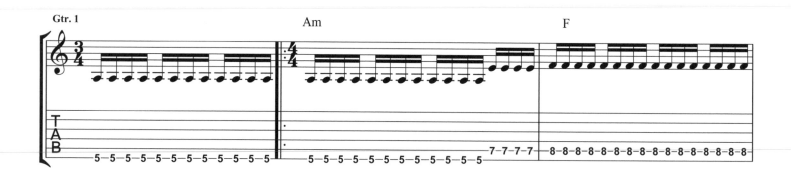

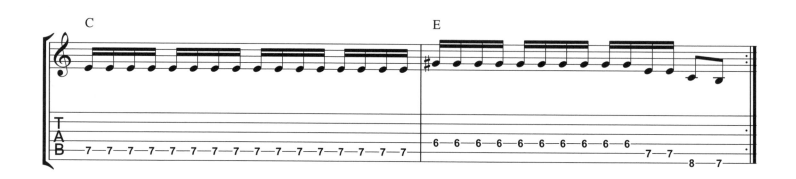

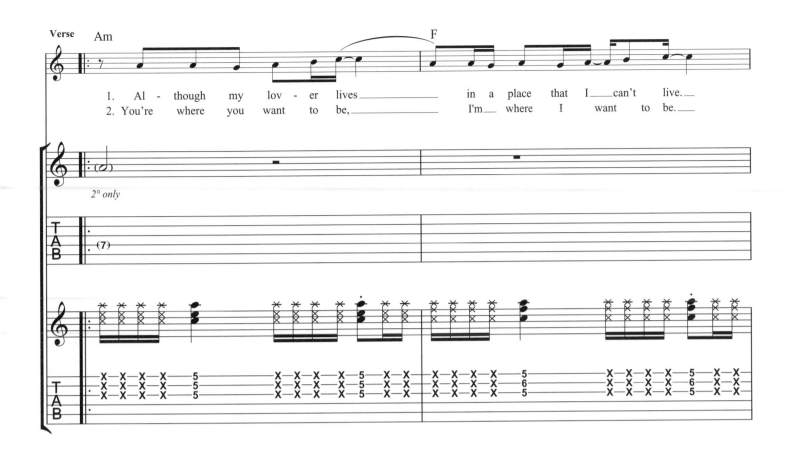

Verse

1. Al - though my lov - er lives⸻ in a place that I⸻ can't live.⸻
2. You're where you want to be,⸻ I'm⸻ where I want to be.⸻

I kind of find I like a life⸻ this lone - ly.
Come on⸻ we're chas - ing ev - 'ry thing we've ev - er want - ed.

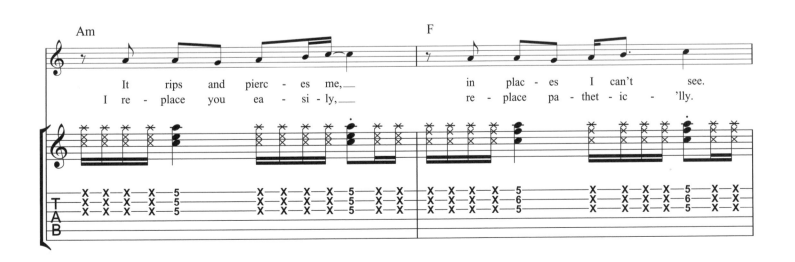

It rips and pierc - es me,⸻ in plac - es I can't see.
I re - place you ea - si - ly,⸻ re - place pa - thet - ic - 'lly.

83

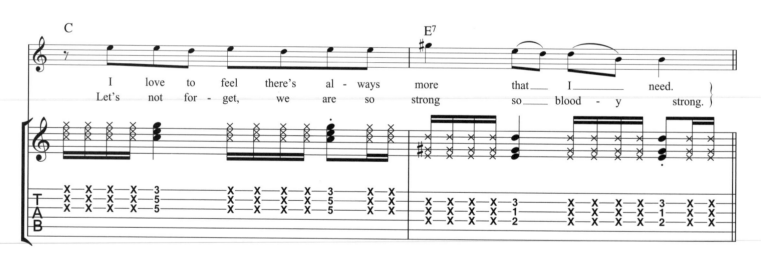

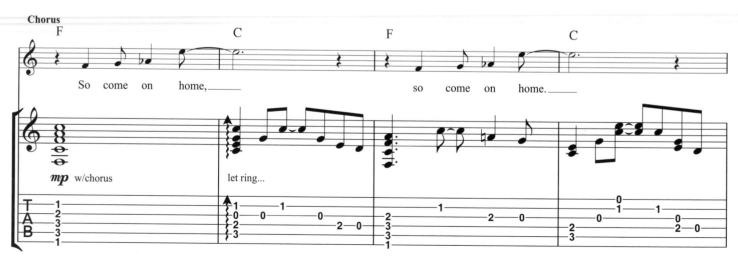

84

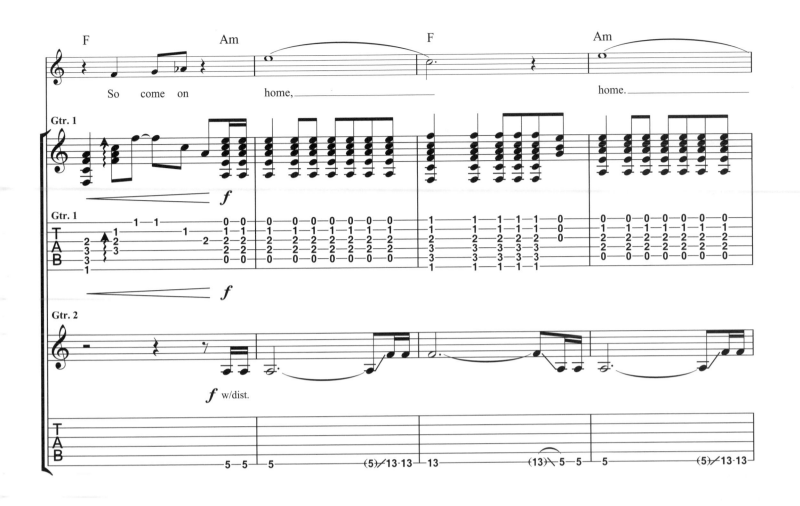

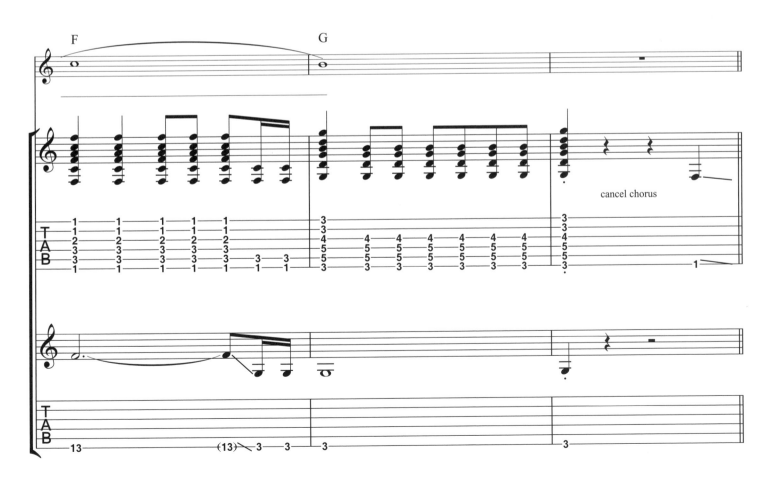

1. Interlude

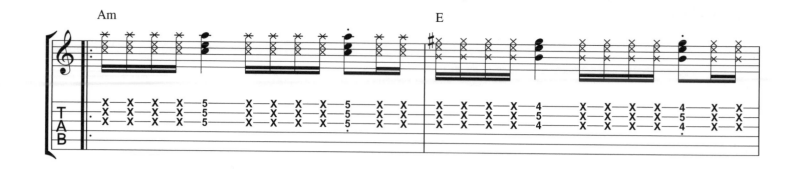

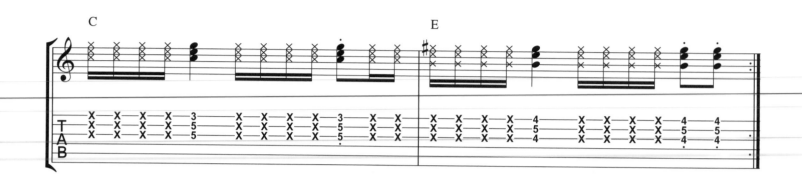

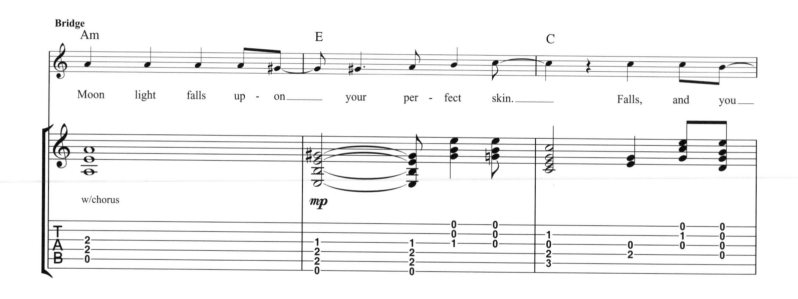

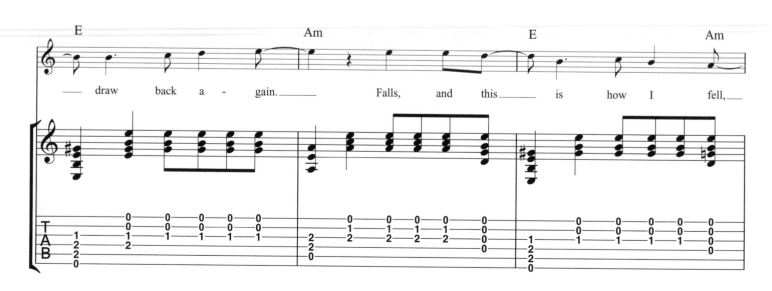

89

40'

Words & Music by Alexander Kapranos & Nicholas McCarthy

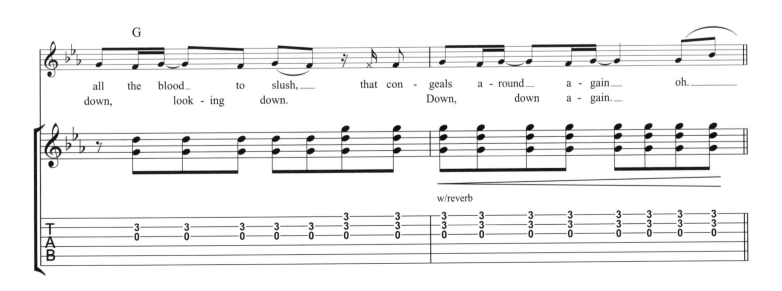

Pre-chorus

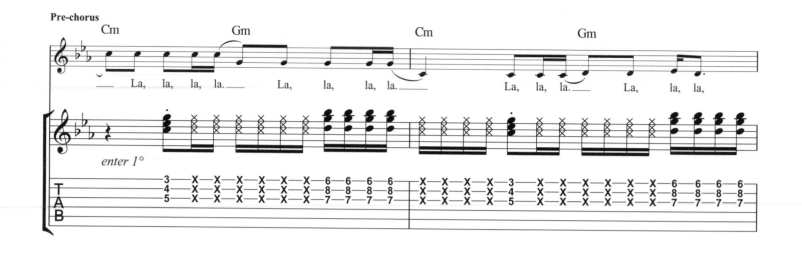

La, la, la, la. La, la, la, la. La, la, la. La, la, la,

enter 1°

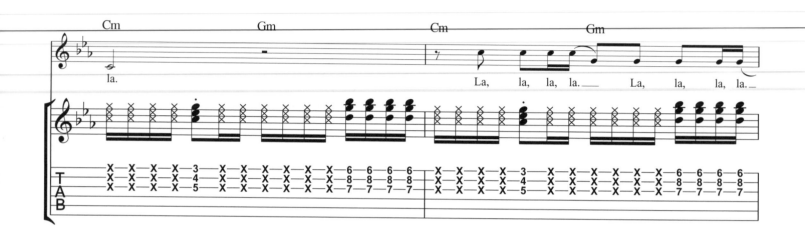

la. La, la, la, la. La, la, la, la.

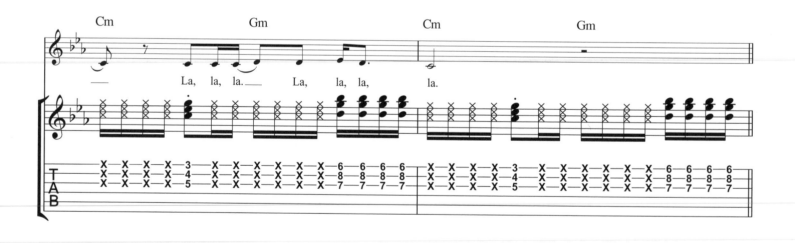

La, la, la. La, la, la, la.

Chorus

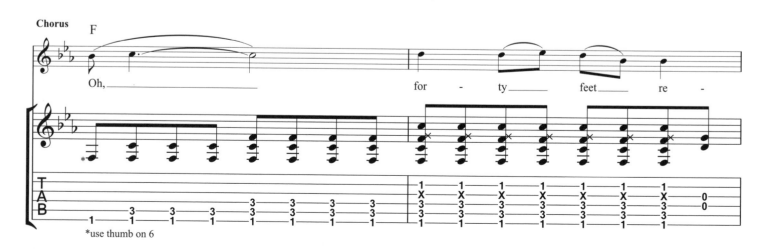

Oh, for - ty feet re -

*use thumb on 6

...Fig. 1 ends

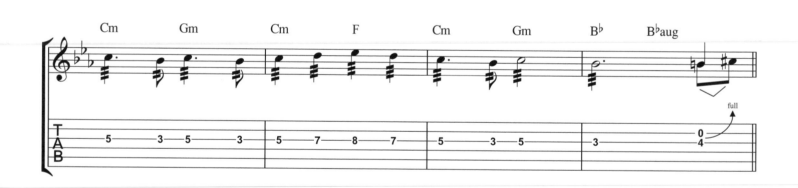

La, la, la, la. La, la, la, la. La, la, la. La, la, la, la.

94

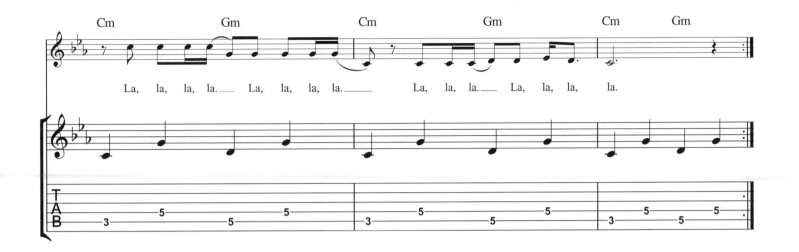

La, la, la, la. La, la, la, la. La, la, la. La, la, la, la.

Chorus

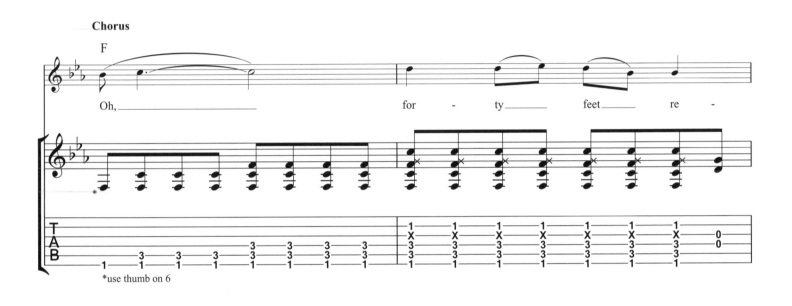

Oh, for - ty feet re -

*use thumb on 6

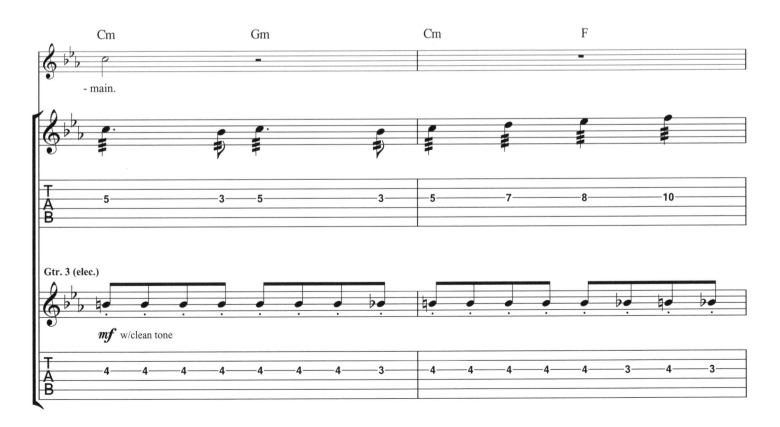

- main.

Gtr. 3 (elec.)

mf w/clean tone

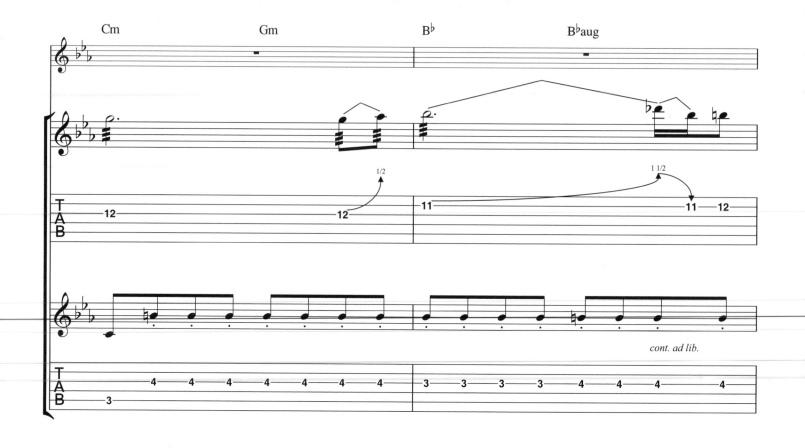

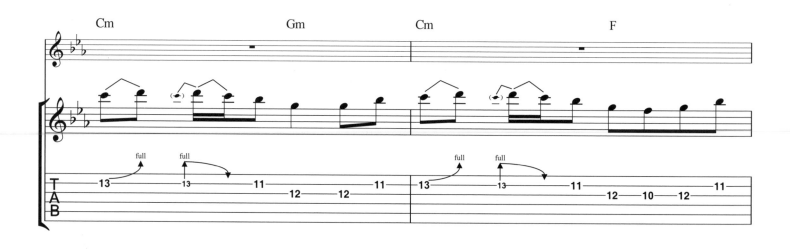

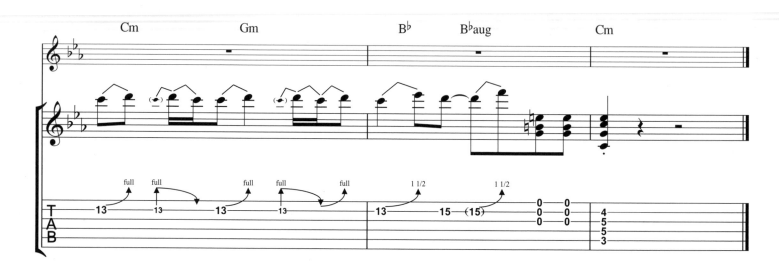

11/04 (53236)